RANDOM

Cozy
CROSSWORDS

Edited by Stanley Newman

Random House
Puzzles & Games

ISBN: 0-8129-3432-6

Random House Puzzles & Games Web site address:
www.puzzlesatrandom.com

Page design and typography by North Market Street Graphics
Manufactured in the United States of America
4   6   8   9   7   5   3

SPECIAL SALES

Random House Puzzles & Games books are available at special discounts
for bulk purchases for sales promotions or premiums. Special editions,
including personalized covers, excerpts of existing books, and corporate
imprints, can be created in large quantities for special needs.
For more information, contact Random House Special Markets at 800-800-3246.

FIRST THINGS FIRST

by S.N.

ACROSS

1 Yodeler's place
5 "Get lost!"
10 Fill roles
14 Windless
15 Numerical goal
16 __ close to schedule
17 1/20/89, e.g.
20 Home room
21 Betz's TV wife
22 Rock bottom
23 Egg on
24 Choir member
25 In jeopardy
28 Uninteresting
29 Tiny colonist
32 Coin call
33 Elvis __ Presley
34 It may be pitched
35 Fine, so far
39 The Rams' league: Abbr.
40 Not at all nice
41 Spring up
42 Give the once-over
43 Polaroid pioneer
44 President __ of the Senate
45 Berth place
46 Job opening
47 Madame Curie
49 Ruin
50 Movie turkey
53 Cole Porter tune
56 Raised, as cats
57 Circus star
58 Chap, to Dundee

59 Give up
60 Nasal sensations
61 Fall heavily

DOWN

1 Corrosive chemical
2 Bowling area
3 Architect's work
4 Dallas sch.
5 Need oiling
6 As good as new
7 Turnpike
8 A.B.A. member
9 California's locale, to Hawaiians
10 Apt. of a sort
11 *The King* __
12 Fly high
13 Take a stab at
18 Concerto __ (Baroque work)
19 Solemn promise
23 Gold-colored
24 Crazy as __
25 Make up (for)
26 Chewy candy
27 Long arm?
28 Not limited
29 Hang around for
30 Mythology branch
31 Indian carving
33 Author's rep

36 Almond-flavored drink
37 South Seas skirt
38 Easy run
43 Beef cut
44 Wire bender
45 Joy's partner
46 Self-controlled
47 Insignificant
48 Got older
49 Floor model
50 Ring up
51 "Render __ Caesar . . ."
52 Fraught with meaning
53 English channel?
54 Hoodwinked
55 Diamond judge

2 HANDIWORK

by Shirley Soloway

ACROSS

1 Falcon feature
5 Singer Redding
9 Ferber et al.
14 Ohio city
15 Tennis star Sampras
16 Metal framework
17 Zest for life
18 Alternatively
19 Artful deception
20 New York resort area
23 On the ___ (fleeing)
24 Majors and Trevino
25 Mouselike mammals
27 Firmly fixed
30 Mail again
32 Saudi Arabia's king
33 Speak highly of
35 Young fellow
36 R-V link
37 Controversial shortening
39 Sound a toreador adores
42 Gibson of *Lethal Weapon*
44 Slips into
45 Perfect match
46 Donkey, often
48 Concert instruments
50 Wool coat
52 Take wing
53 Fam. member
54 Foolish sort
60 Sheepish?
62 Dressed
63 *Born Free* lioness
64 French assembly
65 Past due
66 Stream forth
67 Golf hazards
68 Prayer end
69 Come in last

DOWN

1 Music marking
2 Caron role
3 ___ *Called Horse* ('70 film)
4 Got by scheming
5 Victor Herbert work
6 Spills the beans
7 "___ deal!"
8 Look for
9 Yellowish white
10 Joanne of films
11 Settled once and for all
12 Attorney-___
13 Appears to be
21 Nighttime, in poems
22 Slalom curve
26 Cell substance: Abbr.
27 Preconditions
28 "Unforgettable" name
29 Hans Christian Andersen character
30 Gossipy tidbit
31 007's alma mater
34 Ye ___ Tea Shoppe
37 Skirt slits
38 "Silence ___"
40 Jar top
41 Pulver's rank: Abbr.
43 Palindromic preposition
45 North Carolinian
47 Kyoto cash
49 Norma ___
50 "Mending Wall" poet
51 Pryer's need?
52 Rink footwear
55 Calif. sch.
56 Happy as a ___
57 Seaman's saint
58 Without a warranty
59 Tropical fruit
61 Short snooze

3 DOUBLE TALK

by Trip Payne

ACROSS

1 Falls behind
5 Coffee man Valdez
9 Myra Hess, for one
13 "__ Ben Adhem"
14 Molten material
15 All tied up
16 Eddie Cantor tune of '26
19 Breath-freshener brand
20 Using staff facilities
21 Genesis character
23 Flue powder
24 Go separate ways
27 Frequent title beginning
29 Skirt features
32 Nabokov novel
33 Long look
35 "What's in __?"
37 Senior golf star
40 Where the Owl and the Pussycat went
41 Barely defeated
42 Links standard
43 Quick-witted
45 Enjoy a smorgasbord
46 Juno, to the Greeks
47 Arty New Mexico town
49 Confirmation or baptism
51 Cause
54 Theater district
58 Fifties Kenyan uprising
60 Alternatively
61 Harris storyteller
62 Jogger's gait
63 Makes a sheepshank
64 Walked on
65 Saint feature

DOWN

1 Chem-class locales
2 "Rock-__ baby . . ."
3 *Wheel of Fortune* daytime host
4 Math grouping
5 Holyfield punch
6 Tropical fruit
7 "__ home is his castle"
8 Tex-Mex treats
9 Making a premiere
10 Hertz rival
11 Unimportant
12 Come to a stop
14 *Amahl and the Night Visitors* composer
17 Hankering
18 Kids' drink
22 Stock unit
24 Bloc agreement
25 Kind of committee
26 Mrs. Gorbachev
28 Eat away at
30 Brownish gray
31 False charge
33 Fifties-music revival group
34 Candice's dad
36 Poet Pound
38 Franc portions
39 Calls it a day
44 Cultured food
46 Physical condition
48 More angry
50 "Open 9 __ 6"
51 Indonesian island
52 Put-on
53 Verne protagonist
55 Pisa dough
56 Hammer or hacksaw
57 "__ bigger and better things!"
58 Happened upon
59 Blossom-to-be

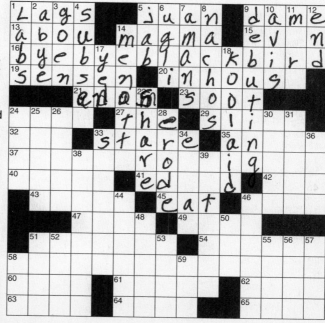

4 WHAT TIME IS IT?

by Mel Rosen

ACROSS

1 Melville madman
5 Everglades bird
9 Director __ Lee
14 Doll's word
15 Chunk-light fish
16 Spud
17 Fifties TV mayor
20 Casual footwear
21 Yes, to Yvette
22 Go one better
23 Hog haven
24 Swimsuit part
26 Throws out a line
29 Bring on board
31 Machine part
34 Abdul-Jabbar's alma mater
35 Fifties TV clown
38 Getz or Musial
39 Texas NFLer
40 Rock's partner
41 Fifties TV marionette
43 Pesky insect
44 Many mos.
45 Transgressions
46 Byron and Browning
47 What RNs dispense
48 Heavenly body
49 Chairman of the '50s
51 "This __ fine how-do-you-do!"
54 Residences
58 Fifties TV host
61 *The Addams Family* star
62 Herbert sci-fi classic
63 Analogy phrase
64 In an irritable mood
65 Part of USA
66 Enjoy gum

DOWN

1 Fuse units
2 Sound of amusement
3 Evil Idi
4 Orchestra's place
5 NATO member
6 Kramden's workplace
7 Sondheim's __ *the Woods*
8 Elephant Boy star
9 R-V center?
10 Ristorante course
11 "Tell __ the judge!"
12 Hang on to
13 Go astray
18 Diner sign
19 Bibliophile's pride
25 Confederate soldier
26 Easy and comfortable
27 Audition attendee
28 Side dishes
29 Heavenly headgear
30 Vexed
31 Genetic copy
32 __ once (suddenly)
33 Turns to slush
35 Will addition
36 Pride member
37 Well-suited for the workplace
42 Fashion monogram
46 Alehouses
47 "Strain the facts __ the rules": Tolstoy
48 Fencer's choice
49 Think over
50 P.M. periods
52 Malt-shop order
53 Hallelujah, I'm __!
55 Reception aid
56 Feminine suffix
57 Revue, e.g.
58 Baseball club
59 Whichever
60 Unspecified person

TWAIN TIME

by Mel Rosen

ACROSS

1 ASCAP rival
4 Thompson of *Family*
8 Major-__ (steward)
12 Get wind (of)
13 *Joie de vivre*
14 Wear away
16 Cuts prices on
18 Boys, in Barcelona
19 Mork's planet
20 Hungry feeling
21 Does fingerpainting
22 Cake finish
24 Biggers' detective
25 Soccer-shoe features
27 Hoarding cause, perhaps
31 Runs easily
32 Armor flaw
33 Peas purchase
34 Like __ of bricks
35 Rich cake
36 Mideast missile
37 Part of TGIF
38 Wanders about
39 Battle strategy
40 Was nurturing
42 Spread (out)
43 Sharif of films
44 Salad-dressing bottle
45 *Charlie's Angels* name
48 Sand and such
49 Came upon
52 Keep __ to the ground
53 Brand-name's protection
55 Pile up
56 Called up

57 Allegro con __
58 Midmonth day
59 Conversation filler
60 Pedigree org.

DOWN

1 Put up with
2 Night Court actress
3 Rub the wrong way
4 Family cars
5 Beside
6 Deputy __ (cartoon canine)
7 Hoofer Miller
8 Hamlet's land
9 Get situated
10 "__ Lisa"
11 Fragrance

12 Medical-insurance co.
15 Ending for host or heir
17 Barbecue adjuncts
21 Was outstanding
23 Columnist Herb
24 Promissory notes
25 Assertion
26 Numbers game
27 Minimal evidence
28 Musical notation
29 Measuring device
30 All over
32 Deal with

35 Synagogue scroll
36 Trig ratio
38 Casual comments
39 Fry lightly
41 Roman odist
42 Latter-day icebox
44 Construction-site sight
45 Musical notes
46 Thumbs-down voter
47 Scanned through
48 Mardi __
50 Author Ambler
51 WBC result
53 Numerical prefix
54 Finance deg.

6 GLOBAL GEOMETRY

by Randy Sowell

ACROSS

1 Borders on
6 Sail support
10 Hard journey
14 Seasonal song
15 Lebanon's locale
16 Slow flow
17 London landmark
20 Pep up
21 Everlasting
22 Presidential prerogative
23 Actor Beatty
24 Nagging pain
27 __ Vegas
29 Big bankrolls
33 Bikini top
34 Author Cornelia __ Skinner
36 Small piano
38 Mysterious Atlantic region
41 Furry fish-eaters
42 Monopoly payment
43 Connecticut collegian
44 High schooler
45 Smidgen
46 Allison of '50s TV
47 Snake with a squeeze
49 Christie's *Postern of __*
52 In the wrong role
56 Charge in court
60 Cook crossed it in the 1770's
62 Defeat soundly
63 Topnotch
64 Sour expression
65 They may be split

66 __ *to Morocco*
67 Watered the lawn, perhaps

DOWN

1 Part of a French play
2 *Green Acres* structure
3 Russian river
4 Nine-__ shift
5 Dred Scott, e.g.
6 Louisiana's state flower
7 Stubborn-mule link
8 Warning devices
9 Esthetic discernment
10 Travel agent's offering
11 Chestnut horse
12 Old Testament book
13 Boat part
18 Allow
19 Proof-ending initials
24 Monastery head
25 Minotaur's home
26 Author Bret
28 Seneca's stars
29 Finish first
30 *Look Back in __*
31 Perry's aide
32 Toklas' colleague
34 __ *Man Flint*
35 Football scores: Abbr.

36 Moral wrong
37 Butter portion
39 Chess pieces
40 Visibly embarrassed
45 Arm art
46 "I will __ evil . . ."
47 Watering hole
48 Pianist Levant
50 Fly-ball's path
51 Actress Van Devere
52 Stable parent
53 Privy to
54 Poker variety
55 Abyssinians and Burmese
57 Tops a cake
58 Cheerfulness
59 Nonsocial sort
61 ". . . partridge __ pear tree"

7 CALLING COSTNER

by Richard Silvestri

ACROSS

1 The West had one
5 Otherwise
9 Astor's wares
14 The third man
15 Sea swallow
16 *Cats* inspiration
17 Sherwood Forester
19 Soda-bottle size
20 Pupil's chore
21 *North by Northwest* star
23 Pick-me-up
26 Tongue-lash
28 Handcuff
31 Kitchen utensils
33 Styling shop
34 Actress Burstyn
36 Mr. DiMaggio
37 Big name in basketball
38 Pine product
39 Isolated
40 In the manner of
41 Alacrity
42 Maine senator
43 Painter Thomas Hart __
45 How ships may run
47 Our Gang girl
48 Film holder
49 Actress Burke
51 Late-night TV host Bob
56 Hold accountable
58 Sherwood Forester
61 Grounds for a medal
62 Devastate
63 Opposition prefix
64 Textile workers
65 Drop
66 Take ten

DOWN

1 Poet Sandburg
2 Large woodwind
3 Cotillion attendees
4 Wallach and Whitney
5 Kind of pride
6 Summer sign
7 Hit-show letters
8 Winds down
9 One with a large food bill
10 Donahue of *Father Knows Best*
11 Sherwood Forester
12 Boot part
13 Orch. section
18 Pitcher Ryan
22 Colorado high spot
24 Heads for the hills
25 Satellite of '62
27 Spoke monotonously
28 Sent away
29 Sherwood Forester
30 "I should say __!"
32 Spotted
33 Stick it in your ear
35 Feudal lord
38 Attacked
39 Bud's buddy
41 Cries out
42 Use crayons
44 Seismic disturbance
46 Eat one's words
50 Bushy hairdo
52 Magi's guide
53 Maintain the piano
54 New Testament book
55 Vaudeville routine
56 Hanes competitor
57 Set (down)
59 Daiquiri need
60 VI halved

8 BASEBALL SUCCESSES

by Mel Rosen

ACROSS

1 Watered-down
5 Canyon of the comics
10 Carpet style
14 Presley's middle name
15 Out-and-out
16 Evening hour
17 Succeed without swinging?
19 Blues singer James
20 Transparencies
21 *Rhoda* star
23 Director Brooks
24 Must, informally
25 Get a move on
29 Toto's creator
30 Nay neutralizer
33 Choir members
34 Abby, to Ann
35 Economist Smith
36 Carrying a grudge
37 Impress indelibly
38 Beer-label word
39 "You must remember __"
40 Zillions of years
41 Splits up
42 __ Ridge, TN
43 Parting word
44 Potato-chip alternatives
45 Civil-rights leader Medgar
47 Joanne of films
48 Asian temple
50 Gives VIP treatment to
55 Like crazy
56 End up succeeding?

58 White as a sheet
59 Hope or Jessica
60 Step __ (hurry)
61 "No ifs, __, or buts!"
62 Not broadside
63 Vet patients

DOWN

1 Radner character
2 Rock star Clapton
3 Top-rated
4 Make a sweater
5 __ Island (Big Apple borough)
6 Beach need
7 Greek vowels
8 Kilmer of *The Doors*
9 Gray dog
10 Hagar's pooch
11 Score a lode of runs?
12 Penny, perhaps
13 Transmission choice
18 Appoints
22 24-hour cash source: Abbr.
24 Picks up
25 Is forced
26 Oahu greeting
27 Get a whiff of success?
28 Stocking stuffers
29 Safari boss
31 __ *Win* (diet book)
32 Making __ of things
34 Harness races
35 Jai __
37 Better than awful
41 Cut back
43 Media mogul Turner
44 Immovable
46 Casts a ballot
47 Don __ de la Vega (Zorro)
48 Hemingway's nickname
49 Actor Ladd
50 __ a hand (assist)
51 Flapjack chain, initially
52 Torrid, for one
53 Send forth
54 Salon jobs
57 Hightailed it

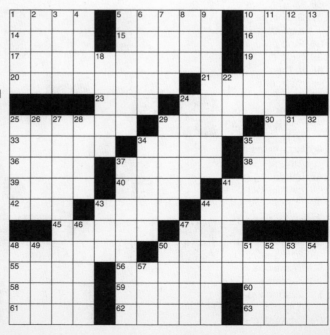

9 CAR POOL

by Randy Sowell

ACROSS

1 Eban of Israel
5 Snake sound
9 Fills film roles
14 Ring event
15 Nabisco nosh
16 National Leaguer
17 "This one's __!"
18 Apple-pie partner
20 Cong. member
21 Rummy variety
22 Bobby of hockey
23 "Harper Valley __"
24 Like the prairie
27 King, in Cannes
29 Bring up
30 John Major's predecessor
35 Liner levels
37 Sci-fi film of '82
38 It has its ups and downs
39 Incoming plane: Abbr.
40 "__ Folly" (Alaska)
43 Richard Skelton
44 Apollo objective
46 Fictional Lane
47 Works at a bar
49 Grass-roots politician
51 Achy or angry
52 __ Tac Dough
53 Date time
57 Author Fleming
60 Third word of "America"
62 One way to stand
63 Delta competitor
64 New York City neighborhood
67 Complain
68 House of Lords member
69 "I cannot tell __"
70 Kennel comment
71 Fine wood
72 __ the lily (overdo it)
73 Tags on

DOWN

1 Scrub a mission
2 Big mistake
3 Farmer's delight
4 Chowed down
5 More comfy, in a way
6 Golf-bag contents
7 Fixed
8 London district
9 Lunch for Bugs
10 Blonde shade
11 Cool it
12 Easy run
13 Kid's pop
19 Trip for Mom, maybe
21 Corning's concern
25 "A mouse!"
26 They may be dire
28 Unfriendly
31 __ d'oeuvres
32 Western lizard
33 Looked at
34 Steiger and Stewart
35 Clammy
36 Slangy suffix
37 Ark arrivals
41 Bring out
42 Ale relative
45 Filbert, e.g.
48 Go wrong
50 Prolonged account
51 Refused to go
54 Shower time
55 Oscar, e.g.
56 Americans, to Brits
57 "Let __" (Beatles tune)
58 Ishmael's skipper
59 Pianist Peter
61 Woodland creature
65 __ vivant
66 Yale student
67 Finance deg.

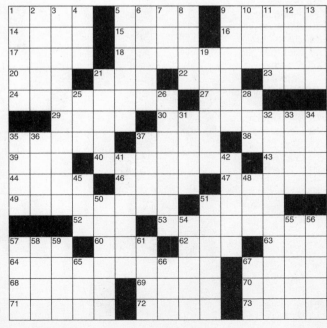

ACROSS

1 Watch the grandchildren
4 Etchers' needs
9 Walked through water
14 Excessively
15 Riveter of song
16 More frosty
17 Charged atom
18 Comedian born 2/2
20 True-blue
22 Round: Abbr.
23 Sub weapon
26 Unstressed vowel sounds
30 Not to be believed
32 Card game
34 Funnyman Murray
36 Did cobbler's work
38 Twine fiber
39 Actor Ray
41 Up to now
43 Sleuth Wolfe
44 Castle defenses
46 Student's jottings
48 Just published
49 Ran away
51 Sign of spring
53 Overly ornate
55 "___ to Watch Over Me"
58 Declare to be true
60 Taj ___
61 Actor born 2/18
67 *Wheel of Fortune* purchase
68 Nostalgic tune
69 Less encumbered
70 Digital-watch type: Abbr.
71 *Revenge of the ___*
72 Tex-Mex treats
73 Soapmaker's need

DOWN

1 Circus prop
2 Ten grand
3 Actor born 2/26
4 Naive
5 Bill's partner
6 Doctrine
7 Computer storage device
8 Highway rigs
9 Macbeth trio
10 Essen exclamation
11 Gaming cube
12 Election suffix
13 AMA members
19 Theater section: Abbr.
21 LAPD alert
24 Twosomes
25 Synthetic fabric
27 Farm wagon
28 Talk-show host born 2/12
29 Long look
31 Clear the windshield
33 Leisurely
34 Doorway part
35 Indifferent
37 Takes out
40 Director Preminger
42 San ___, Italy
45 Mexican wraps
47 Cooks on low heat
50 Opera star
52 Teachers' org.
54 Dutch earthenware
56 Mrs. Reagan
57 Omit in pronunciation
59 ___ avis (something unusual)
61 Actor Voight
62 British beverage
63 Nav. rank
64 Barnyard baby
65 IBM competitor
66 Bus. bigwig

PAUL'S PICTURES

by Mel Rosen

ACROSS

1 Kind of excuse
5 Fix socks
9 Govt. agent
13 Comic Idle
14 Lumberjacks' competition
15 Sitarist Shankar
16 Former soccer org.
17 Late-blooming plant
18 Actor Baldwin
19 Newman/Field film of '81
22 Coral island
23 Presidential nickname
24 Out of practice
27 Droop
30 Mideast nation
34 Italian wine region
35 SAG members
37 UN workers' agcy.
38 Newman/Cruise film of '86
41 Poetic nighttime
42 Bank (on)
43 Sotto __
44 Dickens character
46 Shoe width
47 "Phooey!"
48 Salesperson, for short
50 Galley implement
51 Newman/Woodward film of '76
60 Travel widely
61 Plumed military hat
62 Ms. Moffo
63 Part of AFL
64 Cut off
65 Champagne bucket
66 Hankerings
67 Gives the twice-over
68 Anchorman's spot

DOWN

1 Olin of *Havana*
2 Jordanian, e.g.
3 Long for
4 Choosy, in a way
5 Vitamin amount
6 Sax range
7 Sand bar
8 __ *Rae*
9 County Kerry capital
10 Niger neighbor
11 With: Fr.
12 Delightful
14 Slightly improper
20 Thumbs-down vote
21 Bottomless pit
24 Had some standing
25 Show to a seat
26 Office skill, for short
27 Sub device
28 "A poem lovely as __"
29 __ better (top)
31 Not important
32 Single out
33 British poet Alfred
35 Hearty brew
36 Postal-service abbr.
39 Comparatively peculiar
40 Was owed a credit
45 Military papers
47 Old horse
49 Western band
50 __ about
51 Serving prop
52 Native land
53 Uniform
54 Curds' partner
55 Church area
56 Turner and Pappas
57 Some time ago
58 Till contents
59 Carefree escapade

ACROSS

1 Simon and McCartney
6 Corn eater's throwaway
9 Language of the Yucatan
14 Postulate
15 Ms. Gardner
16 Occupied
17 Laugh scornfully
18 Kilmer of *The Doors*
19 Low-calorie
20 Poetic stooge?
23 Barnyard parent
24 It's split for soup
25 African snakes
28 "__ Entertain You"
32 "Later, dude!"
36 *The Hustler* prop
37 Arouse, as interest
38 Remote computer user's ritual
39 Magazine stooge?
42 Think-tank output
43 River in Pakistan
44 Indivisible
45 Jury member
46 Hiccup, e.g.
47 Lemon-lime concoctions
48 Mrs. Nixon
50 Cambridge sch.
52 Actor stooge?
59 Turning point
60 Bossy comment
61 Battery part

63 Acid type
64 Peanut product
65 From the __ (from square one)
66 Expand, in a way
67 Foxlike
68 Slalom curves

DOWN

1 Second ltr. addendum
2 Outstanding
3 Pre-owned
4 Feudal lords
5 Adobe ingredient
6 Vena __
7 Roundish
8 Cinderella scene
9 Pooh's creator
10 Disney staffer
11 Imported auto
12 Arthur of tennis
13 Badminton need
21 Historical souvenir
22 Go __ (rant)
25 __ off the old block
26 Leather variety
27 Martinique volcano
29 Rig out
30 __ profit (make money)
31 Blends
33 ". . . __ cigar is a smoke"
34 *Chinatown* screenwriter Robert
35 Queen __ lace

37 IOU relatives
38 Freight amts.
40 Radio plug-in
41 Scrumptious
46 Cardinal's insignia
47 Makes amends
49 Playwright Chekhov
51 Public persona
52 Guitarist Hendrix
53 Roman poet
54 Big name in cookies
55 Make muddy
56 Poly preceder
57 Spoils
58 __ out (barely beat)
59 Ben, to Hoss
62 Aurora's counterpart

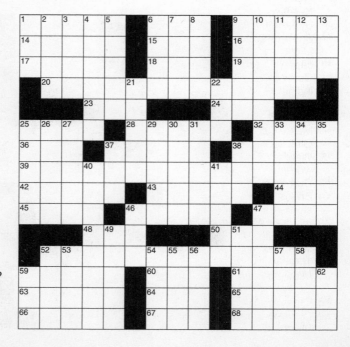

13 CAPITAL IDEA

by Richard Silvestri

ACROSS

1 Former filly
5 Likable Lee
9 Freeway entrance
13 Part of BTU
14 Actress Papas
16 ". . . baked in __"
17 Midwestern capital
20 __ *Haw*
21 Auxiliary verb
22 Nattily dressed
23 Trap material
24 Macabre
25 Copyright kin
28 "Slippery" trees
29 Barbara __ Geddes
32 Due
33 "You're __ Need to Get By"
34 Scope starter
35 Midwestern capital
38 Cover the inside of
39 Mesabi products
40 Make joyful
41 Oink spot?
42 Walkie-talkie word
43 Current 007
44 End of a CSA signature
45 Installs a lawn
46 Hitching post?
49 Turn on a pivot
50 Trifle (with)
53 Midwestern capital
56 Glee-clubber
57 Disney's "Little Mermaid"
58 *Mildred Pierce* author
59 More than half
60 Bar mem.
61 Difficult voyage

DOWN

1 Go, to the dogs?
2 Pot payment
3 Ready for picking
4 Greek letter
5 Mum
6 Packing a rod
7 Equine restraint
8 Miller who dances
9 Hoarse-voiced
10 Each, slangily
11 Little bit
12 Christmas tree?
15 Localized
18 African river
19 Head set of a sort
23 Feel the presence of
24 Immigrants' island
25 Straw votes
26 Stay for
27 Cheap-sounding
28 Bugs' nemesis
29 Sired
30 Poets' muse
31 Irish product
33 Come to terms
34 Vitamin forms
36 Short fictional work
37 Face-first fall
42 Bogus butter
43 Extra
44 Magic Kingdom neighbor
45 Winter fall
46 Steamed seafood
47 Aloha State city
48 Aardvark's entree
49 Bad mood
50 Romanov ruler
51 Steinbeck character
52 Tug hard
54 New Deal agcy.
55 Take steps

by Shirley Soloway

ACROSS

1 Hemingway's nickname
5 No gentlemen
9 Boca __, FL
14 "Too bad!"
15 __ end (over)
16 Be penitent
17 Deep breath
18 Home-repair pro Bob
19 Talks up
20 Understand at last
23 Army bed
24 Implore
25 "To __ His Own"
27 Snack on
28 Least resonant
32 Sire
35 Actor Keenan
36 Smith of economics
37 Commotion
38 Some inadmissible evidence
41 Hula instrument
42 Author Uris
44 Story line
45 Rockies resort
47 Comes out for
49 Farm female
50 Small band
51 Gets even for
55 Ms. Gardner
57 Was suspicious
60 Tomato product
62 Small bottle
63 The O'Hara home
64 Make an appearance
65 TV award
66 Unlidded
67 *Mr. __ Goes to Town*
68 Lunch time
69 Comic Foxx

DOWN

1 No longer chic
2 Totally unfamiliar
3 Debra of films
4 Hardwood source
5 Word of warning
6 Slanting
7 Spanish surrealist
8 Fly in the ointment
9 Chair material
10 From __ Z
11 Improved a bit
12 Not fooled by
13 Roosting place
21 Seventies prime minister
22 Redhead's secret, maybe
26 FBI counterpart
28 Fledglings
29 *Meet Me __ Louis*
30 Benefit
31 Some govt. agents
32 Farm package
33 Heaven on earth
34 Esthetic discernment
35 Corduroy texture
39 Sort of salts
40 Went off course
43 Eur. nation
46 Glenn's title
48 Stair parts
49 Actress Keyes
51 Hertz rival
52 Juice choice
53 Golden-__ corn
54 Get up
55 Imitated
56 Housetop sight
58 On a par
59 Wheels of fortune?
61 Newsman Koppel

15 CARPENTRY

by Karen L. Hodge

ACROSS

1 Shish __
6 Datum, for short
10 G.P. grp.
13 Ms. Trump
14 Protagonist
15 Rude ones
17 Rock bottom
18 PC owner
19 Columnist Bombeck
20 How some fight
23 Cereal topping
26 Conductor Toscanini
27 "Are you a man __ mouse?"
28 Catchall abbr.
30 Five-star monogram
31 Home room
32 Sondheim musical
36 Canadian flier
37 Noise pollution
38 Assistant
42 American industrialist
47 Classified contents
50 Crew-team prop
51 Pro golfer Woosnam
52 Arabian Baba
53 Duplicates, in a way
55 Block deliverer of old
57 Realizer's cry
61 *Andy Griffith Show* kid
62 End-of-semester event
63 Butler in-law
67 Dried out
68 Do followers
69 Fall tools
70 Hallucinogen letters
71 Read quickly
72 Midmorning munch

DOWN

1 The family
2 __ Marie Saint
3 Acting up
4 *West Side Story* role
5 Minor peer
6 Seal up
7 *Entertainment Tonight* cohost
8 Vicinity
9 Oz transport
10 Without __ (broke)
11 Act the pirate
12 Look up to
16 Ritzy shop
21 Inauguration highlight
22 The __ Scott Decision
23 Start to bubble
24 Cartoonist Peter
25 Alliance acronym
29 Closet lining, often
30 Adoptee of the comics
33 *Strangers __ Train*
34 Carry the day
35 Dave's singing partner
39 Muslim leader
40 Oscar __ Renta
41 Green land?
43 Cheer (for)
44 Kitchen tools
45 Reagan cabinet member
46 Popeye's tattoos
47 Parting word
48 Drive away
49 Elevator alternative
54 Suit material
56 Frome of fiction
58 Co. bigwig
59 Shangri-La resident
60 "__ the Mood for Love"
64 Alias: Abbr.
65 __ room
66 Seek to know

16 SONGS OF '72

by Mel Rosen

ACROSS

1 Surrealist painter
5 Oil-bearing rock
10 Cheese choice
14 Stratford's river
15 Eroded
16 Pastrami parlor
17 God: Lat.
18 Gilbert O'Sullivan '72 tune
20 __ spumante
21 Used a fax
22 Dig (into)
23 Pvt.'s superior
25 Organic compound
26 Sammy Davis, Jr. '72 tune
33 One who wanders
34 __ to Utopia
35 African nation
39 Water pitcher
40 Powerful sharks
41 Actor's quest
42 Something __ (unusual)
43 AT&T employee
44 Mint-family herb
45 Don McLean '72 tune
47 High country
51 Genetic material
52 Have life
53 Ray of films
56 Strait-laced
60 Harry Nilsson '72 tune
62 Rate of speed
63 Gin flavoring
64 Buenos __
65 Mortgage, e.g.
66 Longings

67 "__ not amused"
68 Some footballers

DOWN

1 Nursery word
2 Urban rtes.
3 Impolite type
4 Like crocodile tears
5 Spring, e.g.
6 Patriot Nathan
7 Like __ of bricks
8 Fast time
9 Compass dir.
10 Sidles (toward)
11 Passed out
12 Still in the game
13 Clementine's dad was one

19 Mideast port
24 Train unit
26 Genealogy diagram
27 Wolf's cry
28 Two December days
29 Window treatment
30 Oxen handler
31 New Zealand native
32 Marketing-budget items
35 Juice blend
36 Med. facility
37 Et __ (and others)
38 Proofreader's directive
40 Mr. __ (Teri Garr film)
44 Outlaw

45 Vocal range
46 Lindsay's writing partner
47 Worth gossiping about
48 Cast out
49 Climber's spike
50 Cookout residue
53 End in __ (require overtime)
54 Vega's constellation
55 Active person
57 Come down in buckets
58 Topped a cupcake
59 Clothing department
61 Reuther's org.

17 THE BOLD ONES

by Trip Payne

ACROSS

1 Distaff soldier
5 Hosiery shade
10 Box a bit
14 Verdi opera
15 German industrial city
16 Give a hoot
17 FBI agent
18 Gather wool
19 Not care __
20 Brecht title character
23 Not so many
25 90-degree letter
26 Johnson of *Miami Vice*
27 Pub pour
28 "La donna è mobile" is one
32 16th-century council city
34 Platter
36 Becomes beloved
39 Southern sluggers
43 Footrest
44 Vitamin unit
46 Make fit
49 Highfalutin' one
51 Moo __ gai pan
52 The P of "wpm"
53 She's "sweet as apple cider"
56 Extremely pale
58 Classic comic
63 Simpson sibling
64 Not even once
65 Dynamic prefix
68 Preceding periods
69 No longer cutting-edge
70 Iambs and anapests
71 Faxed, perhaps
72 Sportscaster's numbers
73 Take apart

DOWN

1 Shake a finger
2 Marksman's must
3 He played Batman
4 Crusoe carved one
5 *Entertainment Tonight* cohost
6 Arthur of tennis
7 Computer worker
8 Dove's goal
9 Sign up
10 Lasting aftereffect
11 5/30 event
12 Catherine's home
13 Feel contrition
21 Singing syllable
22 "Infra" opposite
23 Craze
24 Lamb's alias
29 Lessee's payment
30 Fascinated by
31 Monroe's successor
33 Invitation abbreviation
35 Hoofbeat sound
37 Statesman Abba
38 Florence's river
40 Rarely visited room
41 Just old enough to vote
42 __ gin fizz
45 Many-faced Chaney
46 Granny Smiths
47 Trace the origin of
48 Gotten out of bed
50 What ewes say
54 Fender flaws
55 Head off
57 Major mess
59 Early cartoonist
60 Nike rival
61 Riga resident
62 Infuriates
66 Beaujolais color
67 __ 60 (acceleration standard)

by Alex Vaughn

ACROSS

1 Enliven
6 Get past the goalie
11 Affectedly shy
14 Senate's colleagues
15 Today's craze
16 Actress Merkel
17 Draw a conclusion
18 Walters spot
20 Smooth
22 "Who __ kidding?"
24 Satisfied sounds
25 Former Belgrade bigwig
27 Redeems, in a way
30 Belly muscles
33 A Bobbsey twin
34 Stick back together
35 Sha Na Na personae
37 Environmental headaches
39 Garage work
42 Tabernacle tables
46 *Wheel of Fortune* buy
47 __ glance (quickly)
48 Bottomless pits
49 Take to the cleaners
51 Topmost numero
52 Ms. Gardner
53 Pennsylvania university town
59 Sylvester Stallone role
60 Corn-chip name
63 Yoko __
64 Mischa of music
65 __ *Attraction* ('87 film)
66 Intuition, plus
67 Wood tool
68 Borg or Ekberg

DOWN

1 __ Beta Kappa
2 L-o-n-g time
3 Breathing hard
4 Software buyer
5 Scope starter
6 Craftspersons
7 Caesar's dog
8 Not fooled by
9 Nothing: Fr.
10 Jazzman Hines
11 Cooking style
12 Brigadier's insignia
13 Go off-course
19 American Legion member
21 Loewe score
22 Part of ETA
23 Dogpatch's Daisy __
26 Light-switch positions
28 Plum variety
29 Board at parties
30 Onassis' nickname
31 Harp on
32 Charlie Brown's sister
35 Some MDs
36 Heathrow craft
38 Little-firm agcy.
39 Chem room
40 Unharmonized passages
41 Hotel staffer
43 High __
44 Race the motor
45 Retiree-payment org.
48 Whoever
50 Family group
51 Sort of sprawl
54 Get ready, for short
55 Grow tiresome
56 Actress Samms
57 Bake-__ (cooking contests)
58 Stick in one's __ (rankle)
59 Doakes or DiMaggio
61 Tiny bit
62 Flamenco dancer's shout

19 KNIGHT TIME

by Mel Rosen

ACROSS

1 Cold period
5 Fast planes, briefly
9 Rural structures
14 Roll-call response
15 Luau spread
16 Single-masted boat
17 Storied sword
19 Entertain
20 Beale and Bourbon: Abbr.
21 Vote in
22 Over again
23 Last name in plows
24 Deck worker
26 Inquisitive types
29 Type of birthday card
32 Maui mementos
33 U.S. artifacts
35 Storage container
36 Lerner and Loewe musical
38 "It's cold!"
39 Like a cad
41 Mailbox feature
42 Sadistic sorts
43 Thin cereals
45 Goes like lightning
46 "Get lost!"
48 Bons __ (witty remarks)
50 Free of errata
51 NFL gains
54 Cookout residue
56 Quest object
58 Mystery data
59 Gilligan's home
60 "__ Want for Christmas . . ."
61 Large group
62 Hammer hurler of myth
63 Fuse metal

DOWN

1 "__ a Lady" (Tom Jones tune)
2 Deli-counter call
3 Circle segments
4 Soup ingredient
5 Rural crossings
6 Cavalry weapon
7 Cease-fire
8 Put in order
9 Eagles' org.
10 Fact book
11 Business conference
12 Small margin of victory
13 Throw out
18 Sly expression
23 __ Moines, IA
24 Gutsy chap
25 Touched down
26 Photo holder
27 Paris' river
28 Malory character
29 Clobber
30 Place on a list
31 Pub game
33 Amo, __, amat
34 Guys
36 Cut out
37 Malt beverages
40 Liqueur flavoring
41 Bottom line
43 Comparatively cloudy
44 Called up
46 Move through water
47 Casals' instrument
48 __ 1 (speed of sound)
49 Cold capital
50 IOU
51 Bush's alma mater
52 Pickle choice
53 Lost traction
55 Vane dir.
57 Not refined

20 BRR!

by Shirley Soloway

ACROSS

1 Mardi __
5 Spheroid hairdo
9 Disaster film?
13 Latvia's capital
14 Prepares presents
16 Out-of-the-ordinary
17 Opening remark
19 In the past
20 San __, CA
21 Minimal money
22 Burn the surface of
23 Rat follower
25 Toward the dawn
27 Under-the-table cash source
31 Upright, for one
35 Barnyard sitter
36 Bombay wear
37 "If You Knew Susie" singer
38 Craving
40 Actress Berger
42 Was generous
43 Least ruddy
45 Dame __ Chaplin
47 Author Buscaglia
48 Barbecue order
49 Grows rapidly
51 Circle meas.
53 Stage pullers
54 Author Ambler
57 Pause in the action
59 Hangs ten
63 Lorre's detective
64 Excludes from participation
66 Admired one
67 Blazing
68 *Born Free* character
69 Be disposed (to)
70 Ltr. writer's courtesy
71 Forest dweller

DOWN

1 Hold tight
2 Chinese-restaurant freebie
3 Matured
4 Native-born Israelis
5 Impress a lot
6 Break
7 Garden tool
8 Broke into
9 Cake feature
10 Country path
11 Whale of a '77 film
12 Mr. Gynt
15 Sp. miss
18 Author Philip et al.
24 Pull __ one (try to cheat)
26 Health club
27 Armada members
28 Permit access to
29 Defeated one's cry
30 Curtain fabric
32 In any way
33 Innovative
34 Black-and-white snacks
37 "__ talk?": Rivers
39 Sneezing cause, maybe
41 Whistle blowers
44 Emulate Killy
46 Take down a peg
49 Blue cartoon characters
50 Gratified
52 __ Romeo (auto)
54 Send forth
55 Took the bus
56 Take __ the chin
58 *Star Wars* princess
60 Portrayal
61 Circuit device
62 Hollywood Boulevard embedment
65 Last letter

by Wayne R. Williams

ACROSS

1 Made logs
6 Ambience
10 Taj Mahal site
14 Luncheonette's lure
15 Like horses' hooves
16 Bread unit
17 Blood part
18 Football event
20 Huntz or Arsenio
21 Roman playwright
22 Plains Indian
24 Thurber dreamer
28 Pro golf event
30 Sci-fi author James
32 Revoke, in law
33 Comic DeLuise
34 One __ million
35 Capek play
36 Hockey event
40 Extra ltr. addendum
41 MDX divided by X
42 Road hazard
43 Used used candles
45 Make a list
48 Tennis events
50 Part of PGA
51 Full of aphorisms
52 Fanatical ones
55 Boast
58 NCAA semis teams
61 Mrs. Helmsley
62 Nasal sensation
63 Change the decor
64 Single
65 Simpson kid
66 Bk. after Amos
67 Burn, in a way

DOWN

1 Beauty-pageant accessory
2 Vicinity
3 Baseball event
4 Take after
5 Beaver project
6 Selling points
7 Enterprise crew member
8 Cowboy's accessory
9 Mideast port
10 Even if
11 Infant's syllable
12 Sushi-like
13 CIO's partner
19 Sergeant Preston's grp.
21 Rocky crag
23 Bush cabinet member
25 Horse-racing event
26 Bowler's target
27 Leavening agents
28 Actress Strassman
29 Eighteen-year-olds
30 As well
31 UN currency agcy.
33 Commercial coloring
37 Designer Claiborne
38 Sure shot
39 Gift-tag word
44 Unisex
46 Salieri's tormentor
47 N. Atlantic nation
48 Not walked upon
49 Sea plea
51 Soft cheese
53 Hendrix's hairdo
54 Leopold's colleague
56 Till contents
57 Walk in water
58 Watch pocket
59 Ms. Lupino
60 Negative conjunction
61 Director Jean-__ Godard

by Trip Payne

ACROSS

1 Legume holders
5 Après-ski spot
10 Turn-of-the-century ruler
14 Devilish doings
15 Sports stadium
16 Tropical spot
17 "since feeling is first" poet
19 Author Hunter
20 Gussies up
21 Agent 86's series
23 Authoritative statement
24 Undergrad degs.
25 Prime-time hour
26 Hymn book
29 Trivial Pursuit need
32 __ Paulo, Brazil
35 XIII qvadrvpled?
36 Bearer's task
38 "The Four Quartets" poet
40 *Beasts and Super Beasts* author
41 Parthenon dedicatee
42 Curly poker?
43 Spelling meet
44 Soldier-show sponsor
45 Sissyish
48 Battleship letters
50 Deluge refuge
51 __ living (work)
56 Don't fret
59 More grainy, perhaps
60 Soprano Gluck
61 *Women in Love* author

63 Ladder-back chair part
64 Electron tube
65 "__ silly question . . . "
66 Glass square
67 Sneetches' creator
68 Fine kettle of fish

DOWN

1 Looks through the door
2 Has __ barrel
3 Unpredictable
4 Pivots
5 Rotating pieces
6 *Exodus* hero
7 Language of India
8 Absorb food
9 Magazine magnate Condé
10 "__ Kangaroo Down, Sport"
11 Philo Vance's creator
12 Controversial tree spray
13 Office expense
18 Pre-Q queue
22 Senator Thurmond
24 Worms, often
27 Novelist Wilson
28 Merman or Mertz
30 Memo heading
31 I, to Claudius
32 Jet-set jets
33 "A Shropshire Lad" poet
34 Grand __ Opry

37 Bathday place
38 Greek letter
39 Occupied
40 Use the horn
42 Ms. Retton
46 Golfer's iron
47 Datebook duration
49 Put forth
52 Mr. T's ex-group
53 Shampoo-bottle instruction
54 Bottle parts
55 Geometrician's finds
56 Grate upon
57 Actress Joyce of *Roc*
58 Interjects
59 Is beholden to
62 TV spots

23 HARD-HITTING

by Eric Albert

ACROSS

1 It cools your head
7 Parisian pal
10 Big shot
13 City on Lake Erie
14 Blueprint
15 Dublin's loc.
16 Like a mosaic
17 Soufflé ingredient
18 Use the microwave
19 Round a rink
20 Snoop's motivation
22 LBJ son-in-law
24 Central sections
25 Poodle name
28 Unpaired
29 Pittsburgh player, for short
30 "Get a load of that!"
31 European airline
32 Request
36 On the summit
37 British playwright Joe
39 Consequently
40 In sad shape
42 Tampa clock setting: Abbr.
43 Course length
44 Have vittles
45 Recording label
46 Shed tears
47 Slyly malicious
50 Hue and cry
52 Bow material
54 Katmandu's country
58 George's brother
59 Sea swallow
60 Conventional city?
61 Handy Latin abbr.
62 Sharp taste
63 Milk holder
64 Baseball commissioner Vincent
65 Before, in palindromes
66 Walk of life

DOWN

1 Like __ (candidly)
2 Bop on the bean
3 Singer Fitzgerald
4 Ferlinghetti and Ginsberg, e.g.
5 Parting word
6 Saturn or Neptune
7 Police bulletin
8 Hawaiian isle
9 Ready to use, as a camera
10 *Arabian Nights* bigwig
11 Really steamed
12 British diarist
14 British cash
20 Closet lining
21 Mechanic's tool
23 Become mellow
25 Unwanted fat
26 Tiny speck
27 Alimentary input
29 Small chicken
33 At large
34 Mean man
35 Easy victory
38 *Sesame Street* grouch
41 County in 11 states
47 Foremost
48 It comes from the heart
49 Beatty role
50 Chile partner
51 Slightly ahead
53 Pay attention to
55 Lap dog
56 Declare
57 Behind time
60 *Pygmalion* monogram

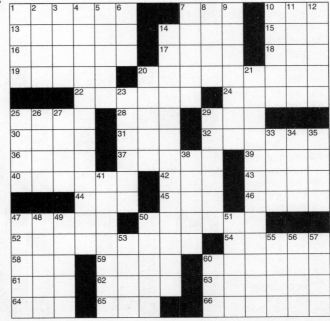

24 VERTICES

by Mel Rosen

ACROSS

1 Fill fully
5 Show amazement
9 *Person to Person* network
12 Brick worker
13 Earthly extremes
14 Move quickly
15 Short of cash
17 Chicken-king link
18 *Much __ About Nothing*
19 Bring up
20 First name in glue
22 Open-hearted
24 Drawer attachment
25 Talks too much
30 Singer Lane et al.
33 Simple Simon's yens
34 Seafood delicacy
35 Litigious one
36 Old hat
38 Brassy Horne
39 Under the weather
40 Nibble on
41 Was helpful
42 Every available means
46 "As __ going to St. Ives . . ."
47 Seltzer-making gadget
51 Fudge nut
53 Small role
55 Major rte.
56 Swear words?
57 Foundation element
60 USO visitors
61 Large antelope
62 Sahara stopovers
63 Sault __ Marie, MI
64 Makes a dress
65 Told a whopper

DOWN

1 Riyadh resident
2 __ Martin (007's auto)
3 One __ customer
4 Menu choices
5 Lots and lots
6 Skin-cream additive
7 Church bench
8 Ancient ascetics
9 Having rooms
10 Peevishness
11 Burn the outside of
12 Extinct birds
13 Worked at a trade
16 Be worthy of
21 Spanish article
23 "Good buddy"
24 Baby bouncer
26 Give rise to
27 Wildcat strike
28 First-rate
29 Audition (for)
30 Korea, China, Iran, etc.
31 Wall Street optimist
32 Eager to fight
36 __ *Gotta Have It* ('86 film)
37 Afternoon ritual
38 "Mona __"
40 Raffle tickets
41 Spray can
43 LAX client
44 Patronized a casino
45 A certain smile
48 "__ Were the Days"
49 Had the deed to
50 Bologna breads
51 Swine
52 Work in the cutting room
53 Stick in one's __ (rankle)
54 Sothern and Miller
58 Señor's "Hurrah!"
59 Skater Babilonia

25 WEATHER REPORT

by Wayne R. Williams

ACROSS

1 Take for granted
7 Foolishly fond
11 Actress Ullmann
14 Slo-mo showing
15 *Topaz* author
16 Hole-in-one
17 *The Invisible Man* star
19 __ Tin Tin
20 Jannings or Zatopek
21 Computer command
22 Part of Cohan's signature
23 Delany and Carvey
25 *My Little Margie* star
29 Tug's offering
31 Drink for two?
32 *Scarlett* predecessor
41 Continental abbr.
42 Gallagher's vaudeville partner
43 Actor Beatty
44 Florida collegians
49 Penultimate Greek letter
50 One on the beat
51 Stroke of luck
57 Visual aid
61 Historic time
62 Midday
64 Digestive-system word form
65 Break in the action
66 Sudden noise
69 Had a snack
70 Peter the pianist
71 Filmdom's T.E. Lawrence
72 Directed
73 Prepares to drive
74 Cleared, as salary

DOWN

1 Moved in a curved path
2 Alabama town
3 Columbus' sponsor
4 Lament loudly
5 Hatterlike
6 Spud features
7 Tropical fruit
8 Prospero's servant
9 Rummy game
10 Horse's cousin
11 Slow tempo
12 More aloof
13 Malice, so to speak
18 Dustcloth
24 Scatter seeds
26 Kind of pride
27 "Understand?"
28 Fancy marble
30 "__ and Hopin'"
32 Precious stone
33 Arles assent
34 New Deal grp.
35 Calendar abbr.
36 One of the ladies
37 Sea dog
38 Rustic hotel
39 Society-page word
40 Graduate deg.
45 Velocity abbr.
46 Adherent's suffix
47 Machine tooth
48 Brandy flavor
51 Statutory
52 Seeing red
53 Opened wide
54 Habituate
55 Child's taboos
56 Vulcan, e.g.
58 Parcel out
59 Norman Vincent __
60 Had aspirations
63 Light gas
66 Explosive letters
67 __ *Haw*
68 Hwy.

26 BIKE RACK

by Randolph Ross

ACROSS

1 Play parts
5 Kipling character
8 Pet-shop purchase
12 Café au __
13 __ Kleine Nachtmusik
14 Figurine mineral
15 Logic
16 Throw for a loop
17 Totally attentive
18 PR representative
21 Big-time operators
24 Actress Garr
25 Pseudonym
27 "Now I gotcha!"
30 __ of passage
32 Burning
33 Up-to-date
34 Make __ of the tongue
36 At this time
37 Most important
40 Draft status
42 The Joy Luck Club author
43 Murrow's __ Now
44 Stock speculators, for short
46 Economist's concerns
53 Slacks style
54 Ring out
57 Thine: Fr.
58 CAUTION: __ WORK

59 Coffee
60 Property claim
61 Writer Kingsley
62 Chop __
63 Nav. rank
64 Kent's coworker

DOWN

1 Hebrew letter
2 Kayak kin
3 "A __, a tasket . . ."
4 NFLer
5 Flew, in a way
6 Accustom (to)
7 High-IQ group
8 Ivy League school
9 Santa __, CA

10 Take to the cleaners
11 Phone no. abbr.
13 Lively qualities
15 Vane dir.
19 Episodic show
20 Norwegian royal name
22 Cheerful
23 Dr. Mead's hangout
26 Basted, perhaps
27 Fuse units
28 Biblical peak
29 French farewell
31 Xanadu rock group
32 Brief glimpse

35 Reeling
38 Do wrong
39 End in __ (require overtime)
41 Just awful
45 Conceptual framework
47 Chip __ (Disney cartoon pair)
48 Avoid restaurants
49 Plumlike fruits
50 Bolshevik bigwig
51 Wipe out
52 Orly bird?
54 Evening wear
55 __ de toilette
56 St. crosser

WORLD HUES

by Mel Rosen

ACROSS

1 Onetime inkwell sites
6 Was in front
9 At the apex
13 Immigrants' island
14 Safety feature
16 NHL team
18 Real doozy
19 Beau Bridges, to Lloyd
20 So long, in Salerno
21 Burden
23 ASAP relative
25 __ Brownell Anthony
29 *Dances with Wolves* home
31 Shake up
34 Happy state
37 "That hurts!"
38 Exotic houseplant
42 CIO's colleague
43 One at large
44 Glacier feature
47 Interstate exits
51 Terry product
52 Wine word
55 Drained of color
56 Vessel of 1492
59 Bar bill
61 Novelist Kesey
62 Some chickens
67 Plant classification
68 Blue __ Mountains
69 Samoa studier Margaret
70 Wind up
71 Commented, cattle-style

DOWN

1 Tyrannical one
2 Actress Stritch
3 Make a mistake
4 They're related
5 Heathrow sights
6 Brooklyn, NY school
7 Clapton of rock
8 Lucy's son
9 Total
10 Upsilon preceder
11 It's in the veins
12 Aft. periods
14 __ of (sweet on)
15 Take down a peg
17 Cut (off)
22 Nostradamus, for one
24 Marmalade fruits
26 Eye problem
27 "Little Things Mean __"
28 Improved's partner
30 New Haven student
32 PBS series
33 Use scissors
35 Virtuosos
36 USSR news agcy.
38 Big hairdo
39 Soloed in the sky
40 "__ the fields we go . . ."
41 Spring up
42 Behave
45 Offered at retail
46 Quite unfamiliar
48 Get along somehow
49 Frat hopeful
50 Had an inkling of
53 List abbr.
54 Corn holder
57 Clementine's shoe size
58 P __ "pneumonia"
60 Apt. unit
62 Spinning-rate abbr.
63 __ *Haw*
64 "Are you a man __ mouse?"
65 Little boy
66 South American port

28 SHIPMATES

by Randy Sowell

ACROSS

1 Le Sage's Gil __
5 Iraqi port
10 Citrus drinks
14 Ready to pick
15 Fields of expertise
16 Noel trio
17 Violin virtuoso
19 Stratford-on-__
20 Actress Mason
21 Tree-to-be
23 Latched onto
25 Police operation
26 Important
29 Slalom curve
32 Repair software
35 Product patron
36 Each
38 Stop __ dime
39 Leave one's seat
40 Of interest to Peary
41 Loretta of *M*A*S*H*
42 Radio spots
43 __ *Rides Again*
44 Yugoslav statesman
45 Somewhat suspicious
47 Look at
48 Ms. Garson
49 This: Lat.
51 Be bold
53 Amusing story
57 Theater district
61 Columbo portrayer
62 *Dallas* star
64 "Don't throw bouquets __"
65 Ice rink, e.g.
66 To be, in Paree
67 What's left
68 Socially inept
69 "__ Me" (Roger Miller tune)

DOWN

1 Hat edge
2 Actress Hartman
3 On __ with (comparable to)
4 Resort locale
5 Kind of metabolism
6 Sculptures and such
7 Gets the point
8 Seldom encountered
9 *JFK* actor
10 Charlotte __, VI
11 British rock star
12 Designer von Fürstenberg
13 Vocalize
18 Chastity Bono's mom
22 Miami's county
24 Topple from office
26 Diego Rivera work
27 Short digression
28 Southern senator
30 Sedimentlike
31 Burned, in a way
33 Bring together
34 Florida collegian
36 Big lummox
37 Hue's partner
41 Went quickly
43 Recolored
46 Annoying noise
48 Football field
50 *George M.* subject
52 Orderly grouping
53 Worship from __
54 __ Hoops star Thurmond
55 Ripped
56 Water pitcher
58 "I __ Song Go . . ."
59 Gull relative
60 Designer Cassini
63 Common conjunction

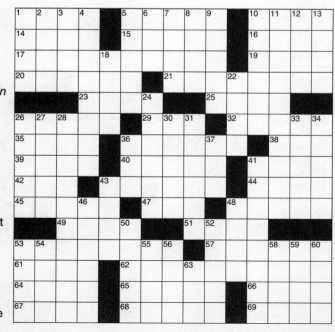

BAR FARE

by Bob Sefick

ACROSS

1 Deep cut
5 *Love Story* author
10 Boone portrayer Parker
14 Run in neutral
15 Hispaniola part
16 Bound
17 Bouncy standard
20 Made beloved
21 Second-place finisher
22 Wine category
23 "__ she blows!"
25 Sampled some soup
29 Any day now
30 Provide firepower to
33 Reactor part
34 Mall unit
35 Lamb comment
36 Sailor's saying
40 __ Grande
41 Has the impression
42 Mental picture
43 Way down yonder
44 Master stroke
45 Promising ones
47 Medicinal medium
48 Mauna __
49 Donkey's uncles
52 End of the instructions
57 With *The,* Salinger novel
60 Puccini piece
61 Boléro composer
62 Glance from Groucho
63 *Green Acres* structure
64 Oboelike
65 "__ we forget"

DOWN

1 Taunt
2 Mideast port
3 Snow vehicle
4 Wherever I am
5 Divvied up
6 Golden-__ corn
7 Hem in
8 Absorbed, as costs
9 __ Abner
10 Wax target
11 Sushi selection
12 Japanese drink
13 Practice boxing
18 Unadorned
19 Wood smoothers
23 Roger Rabbit and colleagues
24 Israeli dance
25 Winter warmer
26 Old Aegean region
27 *Stir Crazy* star
28 Vivacity
29 Clown's prop
30 Lodging place
31 Blue moon, vis-à-vis full moon
32 "Last of the Red Hot __" (Sophie Tucker)
34 Super buy
37 Aloof
38 Film holder
39 Baseball star Raines
45 Not at all cheap
46 Solemn word
47 Pie ingredient
48 Like highways
49 Hailing __ (urban action)
50 Lee of cakedom
51 Agitate
52 Electrically charged
53 Part with, perhaps
54 Genealogy chart
55 Seeing things
56 Boldly forward
58 "To __ is human"
59 Comedienne Charlotte

by Fred Piscop

ACROSS

1 Mardi __
5 Performs like L.L. Cool J
9 Heats and dashes
14 Carson's successor
15 Jai __
16 "__ a River"
17 __-deucy
18 Lily-pad locale
19 Courtyards
20 Sentimental journalist?
23 Pool-table covering
24 Mayo and marmalade
25 Naval officer
27 Belly muscles
28 City in Italia
31 Pro golfer __ Stewart
34 Errand person
37 Former Mideast org.
38 Burden
39 Actor's words
40 Gin flavoring
41 Siamese twin
42 Traffic cone
43 Bridle and primrose
44 Whistle blower
46 Frat symbol
47 Mild acid
49 Book section
53 Baby elephant
55 Walk-on parts?
57 Lettucelike
59 Run like heck
60 Journalist/ reformer Jacob __
61 Followed a circular path
62 Hydrox rival
63 Borge, for one
64 __ around (pries)
65 High schooler
66 Jet-set jets

DOWN

1 Sand product
2 Summarize
3 Lend __ (listen)
4 Versatile veggies
5 White-water locale
6 At __ for words
7 Breathe heavily
8 LP surface
9 TV name
10 Like Dickens' Dodger
11 Rostand hero?
12 Actor Jannings
13 Government center
21 Kemo __
22 McIntosh relatives
26 Letter starter
29 Lye, chemically
30 Bauxite and galena
31 Ode writer
32 Part of A.D.
33 Former Supreme Court Justice?
34 Hodges of baseball
35 Yoko __
36 Boggy area
39 Ode-like
40 Redd Foxx's TV family
42 __ capita
43 Docking place
45 Candy flavor
46 Hydrogen atoms have one
48 Henry __ Lodge
49 Martinique volcano
50 Assumed name
51 Dirty Harry portrayer
52 Mississippi quartet?
53 Thunder sound
54 Prefix for space
56 *Utopia* author
58 NFL distances

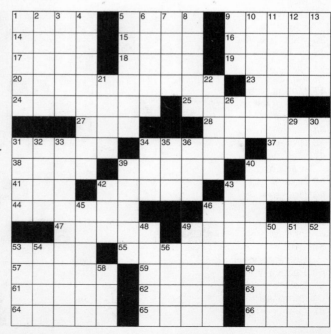

by Max Hopkins

ACROSS

1 Kemo Sabe's trademark
5 High-interest activity
10 Open a bit
14 ". . . __ saw Elba"
15 Word not used in *The Godfather*
16 Big party
17 Riotous brawl
19 Makes a decision
20 Copier chemical
21 Short distance
23 Sennett staffer
24 One being used
26 Barber's need
28 Compass pt.
29 Chatter
31 Pirate's chant
34 __ *from a Mall* (Woody Allen film)
37 Up and around
38 Cremona craftsman
41 Do lunch
42 Sail holders
43 Breakfast fruit
44 Stylish
46 *Batman* butler
48 Fall guy
49 Norton's namesakes
52 Make a new chart
54 Small sum
57 Lamb's mama
59 Atmosphere
61 Get in
62 Durante's claim to fame
64 Girl of the '40s
66 Savage and Severinsen
67 Banquet host
68 Swampy ground
69 Job opening
70 Gave medicine to
71 Billion-selling cookie

DOWN

1 Army healers
2 Odors
3 Where Dole deliberated
4 David and Solomon
5 What the miffed take
6 Mediterranean isl.
7 Strange sightings
8 Barrels of laughs
9 Yak preceder
10 __ Khan
11 Big prizes
12 Vocal range
13 Scrape
18 Slangy assent
22 Some golf tourneys
25 Petered out
27 Anthem starter
30 NFL team
32 Stage success
33 Hosp. locales
34 Put away
35 Film world
36 Place
38 *I __ Camera*
39 Gibson of *Lethal Weapon*
40 Out-of-doors
45 Used an atomizer
47 Painted poorly
49 Cure-all
50 Actress Trish Van __
51 Sound system
53 PR gimmick
55 Treas. Dept. agcy.
56 Headache remedy, familiarly
57 Winds up
58 Yarn material
60 Fundamentals
63 Adjective ending
65 Little stinger

EXPLORERS CLUB

by Mel Rosen

ACROSS

1 Walk through water
5 Mouth off
9 Like the polo set
14 Actress Barbara
15 Dull pain
16 Oahu greeting
17 __ Called Horse
18 NYSE alternative
19 Stair post
20 Alaska explorer
23 Compass pt.
24 Moral standard
25 Lulu
27 Greenland explorer
33 Dowser's tool
36 Newspaper notice
37 Admit frankly
38 *Arabian Nights* character
40 War-prone
43 Office note
44 Mountain lion
45 Vast amount
46 Florida explorer
50 Operatic solo
51 Like some pitchers
56 Guys
59 Africa explorer
62 Kitchen come-on
64 __ instant (quickly)
65 Bookie quote
66 Exodus mount

67 Corsica neighbor
68 Mild-mannered
69 Villain's look
70 Method: Abbr.
71 Puts in a lawn

DOWN

1 Work at the loom
2 Let in
3 __ of a *Salesman*
4 Boredom
5 Swedish auto
6 Top of the mountain
7 Dessert choice
8 More alluring
9 Mental block
10 Grand __ Opry
11 Ticket details
12 "__ a Lady"
13 Bush's alma mater
21 Boston entree
22 Abolitionist Turner
26 Ship wood
28 Oriental sash
29 Coal container
30 Hertz competitor
31 Got up
32 Ladies' club of a sort
33 Freeway exit
34 Bread spread
35 __ *Yankees*
39 Medicos
40 Cry's partner

41 I love: Lat.
42 Eases off
44 Without adornment
47 Rich dessert
48 "Agnus __" (hymn)
49 Would like to be
52 Cyclotron fodder
53 Copland work
54 Finished
55 School furniture
56 Church service
57 "__ go bragh!"
58 Not a soul
60 Captures
61 Small fly
63 Ginnie __ bonds

33 COUNTS

by Mel Rosen

ACROSS
1 "__ Lisa"
5 Abraham's wife
10 Cry loudly
14 Roberts of Tulsa
15 Wear gradually
16 Lebanon's locale
17 Anger, pride, etc.
20 Trifle (with)
21 Old oath
22 Balances evenly
23 Historical periods
24 Imported autos
25 Argentina steppes
28 Business transaction
29 "Telly" network
32 Cancel a mission
33 Layer of paint
34 Court statement
35 Athos and company
38 Heavy weights
39 Mars' counterpart
40 Ledger entry
41 Mos. and mos.
42 Singer Kristofferson
43 __ Berry Farm
44 Put on an act
45 Eye coverings
46 Tests metal
49 Hollywood Boulevard crosses it
50 Binet's concerns
53 Grist for De Mille
56 Essential point
57 Art stand
58 Revue piece
59 Work units
60 Indigent
61 Recipe amts.

DOWN
1 The lion's share
2 Sandwich snack
3 Dark blue
4 Potent potable
5 Marsh plants
6 Fields of expertise
7 Byway
8 Tack on
9 Companion/ assistant
10 Supporting factor
11 Sale caveat
12 Bordeaux or Beaujolais
13 Glasgow gal
18 Bring to naught
19 Cry of pain
23 __-ski outfit
24 Nestlings' noses
25 Hamburger unit
26 Can't stand
27 Pre-noon times
28 Vitamin amounts
29 Declared holy
30 Toulouse topper
31 Playbill listings
33 Radium discoverer
34 Cancún cash
36 Skilled shots
37 Kind of bicycle
42 Boxing result
43 Good-hearted
44 Hard data
45 Like some paper
46 "Ma, He's Making Eyes __"
47 Omen observer
48 Hidden obstacle
49 Posy holder
50 Printer's purchases
51 Stick it in your ear
52 Atl. speedsters
54 Dogpatch's Daisy __
55 Superlative suffix

34 HARDWARE

by Richard Silvestri

ACROSS

1 Curved letters
6 Ego
10 Ring rocks
14 Monetary gain
15 Word form meaning "thought"
16 Came to earth
17 Soft hat
18 In the vicinity
19 ___ 18 (Uris novel)
20 Wolfed down
21 Storm phenomenon
24 Burton's birthplace
26 "Uncle" of early TV
27 Highwayman
29 Macbeth's title
31 Whitish stone
32 Adventuresome
34 Acknowledge applause
37 Astrodome gridder
39 Moving vehicle
40 Beetle Bailey's boss
42 Actress Harris
43 Throws out
46 Hill's partner
47 Head off
48 Knocked for a loop
50 Pygmalion product
53 Turbaned seer
54 Laundress
57 Baton Rouge campus
60 ". . . ___ forgive those . . ."

61 First name in whodunits
62 Turner and Louise
64 Ollie's pal
65 Latvia's capital
66 Stinker
67 Some brooders
68 Get top billing
69 Register for

DOWN

1 Mediterranean isle
2 Tallow source
3 Eccentric
4 Palindromic preposition
5 Come to terms
6 Hole in your head
7 Paradise

8 Heavy metal
9 Boxer George
10 Take a chance
11 Mr. Ness
12 Metric prefix
13 Union member?
22 Bovine bunch
23 Circus trio
25 Up to the task
27 Leeway
28 *Andy Griffith Show* kid
29 Brief treatise
30 Subtle indication
33 Assert
34 Three-sided snack
35 Make eyes at
36 Garden bane
38 Show with sketches

41 *Bonanza* brother
44 They give a hoot
45 "I never ___ purple cow"
47 European capital
49 Yankee Hall-of-Famer
50 Buckle starter
51 Try a tidbit
52 Nile dam
53 Mudslinger's specialty
55 Court order
56 Ms. Korbut
58 Letter encl.
59 Computer owner
63 Electrovalent atom

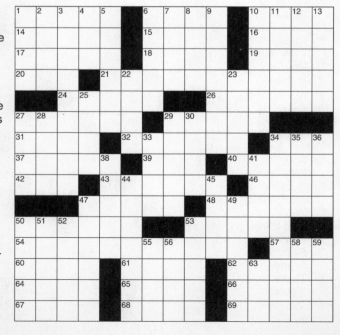

by Trip Payne

ACROSS

1 River in Spain
5 *M*A*S*H* star
9 Bring in crops
13 Villainous expression
14 Black and Baltic
15 Author Seton
16 Arachnid of song
19 Forest females
20 Cowardly types
21 Paramedic: Abbr.
22 Summertime cooler
23 Sidelong look
27 Soak up
29 Tommy of Broadway
31 Galley paddle
32 Prepared to drive
34 "My Way" composer
35 Hornblower of rhyme
39 Martin's nickname
40 Game-show groups
41 Not quite right
42 Plate officials
44 Attractive person
48 Name of three presidents
50 Motherly attention, briefly
51 Yoko __
52 Fast tempo
55 Guzzlers
56 Runner of rhyme
60 Roundish shape
61 Olympian Korbut
62 Prides' pads
63 Moistens
64 Be patient
65 Foil alternative

DOWN

1 Cover with earth
2 Harasses
3 Actor Alejandro et al.
4 Scepter topper
5 TV's Gomez Addams
6 Diminished by
7 Journal pages
8 Give homework
9 Mikhail's wife
10 Finish off
11 Mate's reply
12 Duffer's goal
13 Front of an LP
17 Sanford of *The Jeffersons*
18 Soccer great
22 Guitar ridge
24 Not well-to-do
25 Soap unit
26 Historic time
28 Herr von Bismarck
29 Deep winds?
30 Bone __ (study)
33 Teen heartthrob Johnny
34 Not to mention
35 "__ is but a dream"
36 Hard facts, for short
37 Like sapsuckers' bellies
38 Political group
39 Shepherd or schnauzer
42 Tangelo variety
43 Laid-back
45 Edd Byrnes role
46 All-inclusive
47 Pasadena-parade posies
49 Singer Lou
50 Pay for dinner
53 First name in scat
54 Leslie Caron musical
55 Something easy
56 "That's amazing!"
57 Second name?
58 Scarf down
59 __ de France

36 ELEMENTARY

ACROSS

1 Fur piece
5 Flexible armor
9 The Babe's sultanate
13 __ close to schedule
14 Country singer Travis
15 Othello's adversary
16 Top-rated
17 Starlike flower
18 Corner sign
19 Get things out in the open
22 Swelled head
23 How some try
24 Do the pots
26 Bank jobs
29 Newsman Vanocur
32 Drum's partner
35 Paint layer
37 Bucks
38 Onassis' nickname
39 Pet rodents
41 See the point of
42 Greene of *Bonanza*
44 Right-hand person
45 On a cruise
46 Prepares for prayer
48 Mideast desert
50 Cooks, in a way
52 Of an eye part
56 Pullman, e.g.
58 Levelheaded
61 "Woe is me!"
63 Song of joy
64 Unlikely to bite
65 Carry on
66 Falls loudly
67 Actor Sharif
68 *60 Minutes* name
69 Sudden urges
70 Mouthy Martha

DOWN

1 Prepare eggs
2 __ Gay (WWII plane)
3 Solitary one
4 Foot control
5 Moonshine-to-be
6 Part of AM
7 Mental flashes
8 Hammerstein's forte
9 Family member
10 Retrievers, for instance
11 Excited
12 "__ the morning!"
14 The daily grind
20 Antique auto
21 Goes here and there
25 Important "numero"
27 Writer Ephron
28 Vaccine discoverer
30 "Waiting for the Robert __"
31 Pro follower
32 Columbo portrayer
33 Nutritive mineral
34 Hothead
36 Oxydol competitor
39 Ice-cold
40 Great numbers
43 New beginning?
45 Rickenbacker or Wright
47 Not carefully done
49 Prior to, in poems
51 Lowland
53 Molière's milieu
54 "Be that as __ . . ."
55 Dear, in Deauville
56 Irene of *Fame*
57 King of comedy
59 Light gas
60 A little night music
62 Hog's home

37 TAKE OFF

by Wayne R. Williams

ACROSS

1 Poker stake
5 Got up
10 African nation
14 Old codger
15 Pygmy antelope
16 Latvia's capital
17 Take off
19 Menu listing
20 Correction spots
21 Likes and dislikes
23 Actor Beatty
24 Tissue fluid
25 Wheel-alignment measure
29 Neuwirth of *Cheers*
30 McBain and McMahon
33 Symbol of achievement
34 Take off
36 Oven setting
37 Indicate indifference
38 Characterization
39 Take off
41 Serenity
42 So far
43 Lady Chaplin
44 More incensed
45 Disprove a point
47 __ Paulo, Brazil
48 Concentrating viewer
50 Heel style
55 Ms. Chanel
56 Take off
58 Places of refuge
59 Bring joy to
60 Otherwise
61 Army outpost
62 Became the father of
63 Highland loch

DOWN

1 Dull pain
2 Roulette bet
3 Frat-party attire
4 Ordinal endings
5 One flying high
6 Sampled
7 Art medium
8 Kimono sash
9 Sailor's tote
10 Crunchy
11 Take off
12 Film critic James
13 Boulder and Aswan High
18 Adjusted plugs and points
22 Hemsley sitcom
24 Diminishment
25 Hack driver
26 In the know
27 Take off
28 La __ Tar Pits (L.A. locale)
29 Mandalay's locale
31 Sweet, in Seville
32 Smile derisively
34 Protester's litany
35 __ Scott decision
37 Causes of calamity
40 Japanese metropolis
41 Director Pier __ Pasolini
44 Injured severely
46 Irregularly worn
47 Put into words
48 Strikebreaker
49 Synagogue scroll
50 Arcturus or Aldebaran
51 All tied up
52 Scope starter
53 Prepare salad
54 Washington bills
57 Yale student

38 BASEBALL FILMS

by Mel Rosen

ACROSS

1 Recedes
5 Room's companion
10 WWII date
14 Actress Russo
15 Bowler's milieu
16 __ Lackawanna Railroad
17 Reverse, e.g.
18 Family member
19 Chance to play
20 '89 Costner film
23 Integers: Abbr.
24 Biol. or astron.
25 '76er or Celtic
28 For each
31 Open up, in a way
35 Computer "reading" method: Abbr.
36 Caught in the act
39 Syllogism word
40 '76 Matthau film
43 Natural eyewash
44 Be a sign of
45 Use the peepers
46 Put __ to (halt)
48 Marino of football
49 Comes in second
51 Humorist Shriner
53 Kind of camera, initially
54 '27 Beery film
61 Biblical stargazers
62 Loverboy
63 Tennessee's state flower
65 Ready for business
66 Having no point
67 Salad base
68 Hazard to navigation
69 Change components
70 All-in-one dish

DOWN

1 Bit of work
2 Complaint
3 __ B'rith
4 Cool and collected
5 Parade participants
6 Mixed bag
7 Hebrew letter
8 Bill-of-lading abbr.
9 Textile workers
10 Hostage, euphemistically
11 Instrument for Ringo
12 Affectations
13 Kyoto cash
21 Doone of fiction
22 Old French coin
25 Terra __
26 Yearns (for)
27 *All Creatures __ and Small*
28 Yearned for
29 Actress Verdugo
30 Took back in battle
32 Heavy metal
33 Reach accord
34 "Everything's Coming up __"
37 Say more
38 April setting: Abbr.
41 Window-shopping
42 Snoopy's sister
47 Slapstick missile
50 Planetary paths
52 Sammy Cahn creation
53 Mules and pumps
54 Batman's accessory
55 Maturing agent
56 First-class
57 Fed. agent
58 Bivouac shelter
59 In __ (stuck)
60 Fork point
61 Unruly bunch
64 Wood processor?

by Mel Rosen

ACROSS

1 Sore spot
5 Hot tub
8 Boston NBAer
12 Cozy spot
13 Paid out
15 He raised Cain
16 3/4 of a dozen
17 Tall bird
18 Cathedral area
19 Grand __ Opry
20 Sammy Davis, Jr. tune
22 Judaism's Allah
24 Twosome
25 Ornamental flower
27 Turndown
31 Elementary particles
32 Cartoon creature
34 GI's hangout
35 Large amounts
36 __ with faint praise
37 Not "fer"
38 Compass dir.
39 Ports and such
40 Foil, for example
41 Fox's name
43 Not as well-done
44 Directional ending
45 Added attractions
47 Eurythmics tune
51 Former Mideast org.
54 Some shortening
55 Ease

56 Mean monster
57 Similar (to)
58 Early cataloguer
59 Miss the boat
60 Bump into
61 Ga. neighbor
62 Set-to

DOWN

1 __ Domini
2 Wrap around
3 Abba tune
4 Supplement, with "out"
5 Wild escapade
6 Yellowish pink
7 Magnani of film
8 __ Top This? (old game show)
9 Wax-coated cheese
10 It's enlarging Hawaii
11 Fed. agents
13 Vowel sound
14 Makes an offer
20 "__ Magic Moment"
21 Actor Howard
23 Charity
25 Library stamp
26 Seeing eye to eye
27 Hose mishaps
28 Archies tune
29 Out of the way
30 Antisocial type
32 True grit?
33 Sra., in France
36 Tyrolean skirts

37 Skin-cream additive
39 Toad feature
40 Factory manager
42 Have no obligation to
43 Some shoes
45 "She loves me" scorekeeper
46 Singer Branigan
47 Bridge coup
48 Greet the day
49 Toledo's lake
50 Sailing hazard
52 Domingo melody
53 Bank (on)
56 Switch position

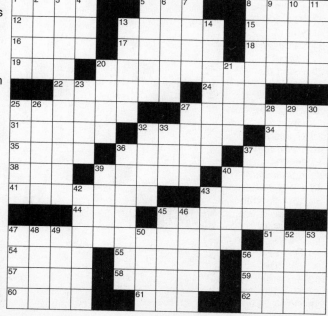

40 ALTERNATE ROUTES

by Eric Albert

ACROSS

1 Itty-bitty branch
5 Say "guilty," say
10 *Green __ and Ham*
14 Whale of a movie
15 Rent
16 Leave flat
17 Ritzy New York store
20 Be a mole
21 Hamelin menaces
22 Pull up stakes
23 Small liqueur glass
24 Guitarist Atkins
25 Utterly hopeless
28 Max of *The Beverly Hillbillies*
29 Book after Esther
32 Haunted-house sound
33 Gymnast Korbut
34 Asian desert
35 '80s police series
38 They're slippery when wet
39 Conform to
40 Rope ring
41 High's partner
42 Cut quickly
43 Lend an ear
44 Comply with
45 Makes a wager
46 Ancient
49 Sweater eater
50 Phi-psi link
53 Centrist
56 Theater award
57 Hawaiian "Hi!"
58 Bewilder with a blow
59 Look to be
60 Not at all tame
61 Lumber choppers

DOWN

1 Sleep unsoundly
2 Stole, for example
3 Revolting
4 Argon or neon
5 Easily bent
6 *Waiting for __*
7 Gulps down
8 Volcano output
9 Racetrack tie
10 Kick out
11 Ms. Lollobrigida
12 Down in the mouth
13 "That's one small __ . . ."
18 Monks' wear
19 Change course
23 Rings out
24 Sly as a fox
25 Felt pity
26 Bramble, e.g.
27 Bread spread
28 Delete an expletive
29 Go lance to lance
30 Overly large
31 American buffalo
33 Go around
34 It'll hold water
36 Poor at crooning
37 Gay and cheerful
42 Bear's advice
43 __ *Weapon* (Gibson film)
44 Computer-telephone device
45 South Africa's former PM
46 Football's __ Alonzo Stagg
47 Taunt
48 Adams or McClurg
49 *Dial __ Murder*
50 Try to influence
51 Visibility problem
52 March 15th, for one
54 ". . . Round the __ Oak Tree"
55 Nutrition stat.

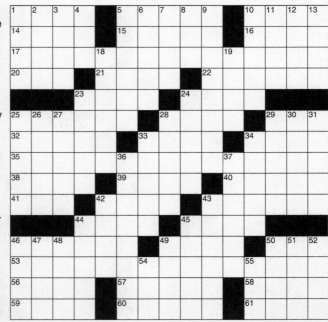

41 GOING PLACES

by Shirley Soloway

ACROSS

1 Sch. at Tempe
4 Dieter of rhyme
9 Ms. Verdon
13 Connery role
15 Author Jong
16 Hard to find
17 Yearbook inscriptions
19 Spanish I verb
20 Tip over
21 Golf gadgets
22 *Moonstruck* Oscar-winner
23 Some makeup
25 Majestic story
27 Lawyers' grp.
28 Eased
31 Church official: Abbr.
34 Repair a tear
37 Mom's brother
38 __ *American Cousin*
39 Dining-room staffers
41 Research room
42 Make a speech
44 Half a Samoan city
45 Flexed
46 Noisy celebration
48 Central mail loc.
50 Nathan Hale's alma mater
51 Office tyros
56 Pats lightly
58 Prefix for dynamics
60 Move laterally
61 Orchestral instrument
62 Geometric intersection
64 Fish-story teller
65 Omit in pronunciation
66 Market rise
67 "Shall we?" answer
68 Boca __, FL
69 Antique car

DOWN

1 Demean
2 Silly Sales
3 Loosen a knot
4 Sun. talk
5 Empty talk
6 More mature
7 Dull pain
8 Mortarboard attachment
9 "Ode on a __ Urn"
10 Launderer's concern
11 Art Deco artist
12 In the neighborhood
14 Canadian cash
18 Smooth-talking
24 Whale of films
26 In addition to
28 Sick as __
29 Lively spirit
30 Obligation
31 Othello was one
32 Free of doubt
33 Dinner-service piece
35 Catch sight of
36 Hoop group: Abbr.
39 Ameche role
40 Meditative discipline
43 Little puzzles
45 __ up on (studying)
47 Cyrus McCormick invention
49 Tower town
51 Characteristic
52 Concerto movement
53 Seer Cayce
54 *Dallas* mama
55 "__ evil . . ."
56 Well-behaved kid
57 Rose's beau
59 Singer Fitzgerald
63 Poetic night

42 ENOUGH!

by Mel Rosen

ACROSS

1 Shopping prop
5 Get off, on the gridiron
11 Banned pesticide
14 Theater award
15 Spice things up
16 Seafood delicacy
17 Put a stop to
19 Pussycat's companion
20 Took the wheel
21 Force forward
23 Jaguar or Cougar
24 Appeals-court rulings
26 Goes bad
29 Knock down
30 Get together
31 Clark's colleague
32 No gentleman
35 Sprightly tune
36 Turn (to)
37 Hailing call
38 Wright wing
39 Quail quantity
40 Norwegian coin
41 Molecular variation
43 Flew like an eagle
44 Afternoon performance
46 Draw on
47 Video-game name
48 Provides comfort
52 Near the center
53 Cease
57 Resembling
58 Heavens-related
59 Nobel Peace Prize city
60 Squalid quarters
61 Prying needs
62 *Pygmalion* playwright

DOWN

1 Friday and Drummond
2 Border upon
3 Get one's goat
4 Put on the air
5 They lead you on
6 Must have
7 Unsubstantial food
8 Catalina, for one: Abbr.
9 Singer Rawls
10 Fire trucks
11 Prepare to rest
12 Wooden rod
13 Spills the beans
18 Hors d'oeuvres holders
22 Actress Farrow
24 __ decimal system
25 Kuwaiti prince
26 Hill's partner
27 Runner Zatopek
28 Close up shop
29 Take a back seat (to)
31 River structure
33 High-grade
34 __-in-the-wool
36 "The Eternal City"
37 Wyoming Indians
39 Funnel-shaped
40 Arboreal Aussie
42 *To __ with Love*
43 Bar seating
44 __ *Family* ('80s sitcom)
45 At an angle
48 Top draw
49 Pocket money
50 Scat queen
51 Pack away
54 Sugary suffix
55 VH-1 rival
56 Sooner than

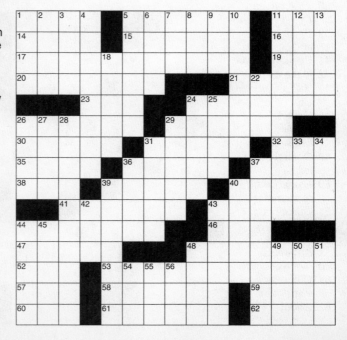

by Shirley Soloway

ACROSS

1 Real money
5 Become blurry
9 Dirty air
13 Racqueteer Arthur
14 By __ (barely)
16 Point out
17 Of limited duration
19 Poker payment
20 Part of TLC
21 __ Na Na
22 Rivers, to Roberto
23 Derisive look
24 Take away (from)
26 Ready to pick
28 Actress North
31 Chem rooms
34 Lee of cakedom
37 Wipe out
38 Nest-egg letters
39 '60s pop singer
41 An NCO
42 Dietary need
44 Put on the market
45 "The __ the limit!"
46 *Butterfield 8* star
48 __ mater
50 Dresses up
53 Roundish shapes
57 Powder ingredient
59 Memorable time
60 When *Dallas* was on
61 Touch against
62 Clam variety
64 Jury member
65 It divides Paris
66 Happiness
67 Actress Lanchester
68 Ship out
69 Makes a statement

DOWN

1 Throws out a line
2 Pale-colored
3 Was all aglow
4 Sheepdogs, for instance
5 Jamie or Felicia
6 "Eureka!"
7 __ *Macabre*
8 Dinnertime of film
9 Less common
10 Satellite-locating system
11 Director Preminger
12 The Bee __ (rock singers)
15 Brings up
18 Ms. Garr
24 College officials
25 "Excuse me!"
27 Greek letter
29 Catch sight of
30 Long swimmers
31 Pick-me-up
32 Oratorio piece
33 Some eyes, so to speak
35 Deli bread
36 Earth bound?
39 Walked over
40 Under the weather
43 Agamemnon's daughter
45 Nest eggs
47 Country dances
49 Last word of "I Got Rhythm"
51 Shouts out
52 *The Sons of __ Elder* (Wayne film)
54 Writer Rogers St. Johns
55 Cagney's TV partner
56 Actress Brenda
57 Finish-line prop
58 Genesis son
60 Took off
63 Country-music cable sta.

44 BEARDS

by Cynthia Lyon

ACROSS

1 Plumb crazy
5 Stroller, in Sussex
9 S.V. Benét's Farmer Stone
14 The Bard's river
15 Big fuss
16 Unanimously
17 Eatery listing
18 Bearded leader
20 Rural sts.
21 Wasn't colorfast
22 Police-blotter abbr.
23 Citric quencher
24 Cereal grain
25 Darth Vader's side
28 Trees akin to cashews
31 Has the potential to
32 Freud's concern
33 Bearded monarch
36 Up
38 Bearded cartoon character
40 Macho type
43 Bearded sibs
47 Thurman of *Henry & June*
48 Squid squirt
50 *This __ Life*
51 Percussion gourd
53 Mineo of movies
55 High range: Abbr.
56 Zilch
57 Paris hotel
59 Airborne Dracula
60 Bearded gift-bearer
63 "Dueling," to "indulge": Abbr.
65 Mr. T's former group
66 Actress Sedgwick
67 Gross
68 Madison vice president
69 "Wait __!" ("Hold on!")
70 Abound

DOWN

1 Felon's flight
2 Past the deadline
3 Judge unfit
4 Responsibility
5 Harper Valley org.
6 Actor Benson
7 Astaire's sister
8 Double agent
9 Funnyman Murray
10 Songwriters' org.
11 Bet middlers?
12 Blow up
13 Buddhist sect
19 Thought
23 Fire wood?
24 Write that you're coming
26 Yule aromas
27 Zillions of years
29 Instrument for an ángel o
30 Bluish
31 La Bohème
34 "And all __ is a tall ship . . ."
35 Doctrine
37 "One __ land . . ."
39 Electric co., e.g.
40 Render a tune
41 Flow forth
42 American Leaguer
44 Harlequin genre
45 Movie-set blooper
46 Grads.-to-be
49 Anti-drug officer
52 Wedding setting
53 Collar inserts
54 Sky's color
58 Chase of Hollywood
59 Worms, often
60 Lose firmness
61 *Little Women* girl
62 Air Force org.
64 Prom locale

by Mel Rosen

ACROSS

1 Ump's call
5 Llama land
9 *Misery* star
13 Singer Guthrie
14 Church area
15 Bring to naught
16 Mr. Connery
17 Low-priority place
19 Owns
20 Love-neighbor link
21 London section
22 Some sandwiches
24 Teachers' org.
25 Roof support
27 Pre-meal drink
32 Meadows' hubby
33 *The Plains of Passage* author
34 Milan money
35 As well
36 Summer spell
39 Abolitionist Turner
40 Genesis character
42 Bridal wear
43 Fake jewelry
45 They make conclusions
47 Like baby food, often
48 Neither fish __ fowl
49 Strike a pose
50 Tenderly, in music
54 "Absolutely!"
55 Lacrosse-team complement
58 Small stitch
60 Ace in the __
61 Diner sign
62 Machu Picchu people
63 Night fliers
64 Wild plum
65 Some votes
66 Tiny fly

DOWN

1 Waistband
2 General vicinity
3 Heavy-rain result
4 Very long time
5 Stage shows
6 List-ending abbr.
7 Croupier's gadget
8 In a suave manner
9 Shorten
10 Last Stuart monarch
11 Yemen seaport
12 L'Etoile du __ (Minnesota's motto)
14 Can't stand
18 __-friendly computer
20 The way things are going
23 French season
25 Appraised
26 Without equal
27 German cars
28 Ring out
29 Hollywood's nickname
30 Hopping mad
31 Destined
33 Worry, it's said
37 Tennis effect
38 Commercial canine
41 Crowing time
44 "Chances __" (Mathis tune)
46 Old geezer
47 Yeats and Keats
49 Caged talkers
50 Joe Young's family
51 It may be square
52 Football great Graham
53 Mrs. Chaplin
56 Jazz-singing name
57 Bird house
59 Not at all friendly
60 Monopolize

46 INSTRUMENTAL

by Shirley Soloway

ACROSS

1 South __, IN
5 Platter
9 At a distance
13 One more time
15 Roman orator
16 Where the grapes are
17 Interfered with
19 Author Ferber
20 Scenery suffix
21 Went too far
23 Kept up the criticism
26 Bandleader Brown
27 Pregrown grass
30 Reclined
31 Oxen harness
33 Circular dance
35 Absorbed with
37 Roebuck's partner
40 Responsibility
41 Operetta composer
43 Water holder
44 Circus star
46 Fully convinced
47 Breathe heavily
48 *Serpico* author
50 DC 100
52 Roll-call vote
53 Beer kin
55 "Quiet!"
58 Fashion designer
60 *Salvador* star
63 Pour __ (exert oneself)
64 Biology branch
68 Amaze
69 Software buyer
70 Sticky stuff
71 Sound-stage areas
72 Be abundant
73 Stack role

DOWN

1 Ebenezer's outburst
2 Swelled heads
3 Antidrug cop
4 Singing Shore
5 CCC plus CCCI
6 Author Fleming
7 Got to one's feet
8 Escort fleet
9 Declare
10 Waste, as time
11 Musical of "Tomorrow"
12 Hits the books
14 High land
18 Get off the track
22 Slaughter of baseball
24 Some evergreens
25 Show excitement
27 Took a photo of
28 Charlie's wife
29 Dismissed from the service
32 Hold on to
34 En route, in a way
36 Used paddles
38 M. Descartes
39 Sp. miss
42 Fame or acclaim
45 Criticizes
49 Don't participate in
51 Descend rapidly
53 Not quite right
54 Singer Lenya
56 By itself
57 "The Man Without a Country"
59 Traveler's stops
61 Medicine amount
62 Some NCOs
65 Wide-eyed remark
66 Furnish weapons to
67 "__! We Have No Bananas"

BIRTHDAYS THIS WEEK

by Mel Rosen

ACROSS

1 The word, at times
4 Scale a peak
9 Pa Clampett
12 "I beg your pardon!"
14 Traffic-report source
15 Opera star
16 Film critic born June 18th
18 Give off
19 Transparent act
20 Okay as food
22 Cairo waterway
24 Zilch
25 Complain in court
29 Beef cut
31 Detective Archer
34 Truth, old-style
35 Animation frames
36 As __ (therefore)
37 What the suspicious smell
38 Silently understood
39 Cuba, por ejemplo
40 Auction word
41 "Do __ others . . ."
42 Taj __
43 Letter carrier: Abbr.
44 Harris' __ Rabbit
45 Mideasterner
46 Mideasterner
48 Sore spot
50 Deer meat
53 Skilled worker

58 Vaccine type
59 Comedian born June 17th
61 Shredded
62 Barkin of *The Big Easy*
63 "What __ is new?"
64 Native Alaskan: Abbr.
65 Claude's cup
66 __ Monte

DOWN

1 Mr. Antony
2 "Oops!"
3 Bytes or bucks lead-in
4 Bank offering
5 Recording company
6 Chemical suffix

7 Swampland
8 Plant pro
9 Actor born June 15th
10 Demonic
11 See socially
13 *Mal de* __
15 Senior member
17 Western spread
21 32,000 ounces
23 Orestes' sister
25 Missouri river
26 Element #5
27 Actress born June 16th
28 Leather ending
30 Mixed bag
32 Showy display
33 Migratory mammal
35 Walking stick

36 Anna's adopted home
38 Airplane engine
42 Bumps into
44 Coll. degrees
45 Holy place
47 Get one's goat
49 Superheroes' wear
50 Have one's say, in a way
51 Greek Cupid
52 Novelty piano piece
54 Rink surface
55 Real-estate sign
56 Cathedral area
57 Coward of the theatre
60 High trains

48 ISLANDERS

by Randy Sowell

ACROSS

1 Piano practice
6 Army leaders
11 Mature
14 War hero Murphy
15 News summary
16 *Pillow Talk* star
17 Indonesian singer?
19 Pub potable
20 ___ Kleine Nachtmusik
21 *For the Boys* actor
22 "A Boy ___ Sue"
24 Pooh's pal
25 Rhyme for fizz
26 "You bet!"
27 Mediterranean actor?
33 Prayer beads
36 Cruise in films
37 Feedbag fill
38 Stay clear of
39 Morning moisture
40 Kind of rate or rib
41 Architect Saarinen
42 Coach Parseghian
43 Left port
44 Indonesian crooner?
47 Short sleep
48 Collection agcy.
49 Brobdingnagian
52 Fictional flying monster
55 *Born Free* roarer
57 It often turns
58 Charlottesville sch.
59 Mediterranean actress?

62 ___ Aviv
63 Make amends
64 Hole-___
65 Whichever
66 Seasons, maybe
67 Word on a nickel

DOWN

1 *60 Minutes* reporter
2 Unusual art
3 *A Bell for ___*
4 Bank sight
5 Comics cry
6 Poultry part
7 Singer McEntire
8 Open up ___ of worms
9 Actor Mineo
10 Small piano
11 First-family member
12 High wind
13 Looked at
18 In an unfriendly way
23 Oregon city
25 ___ Krishna
26 Sweet tuber
27 Rock megastar
28 Work as ___ (collaborate)
29 Cut the lawn
30 Pellets of a sort
31 "Don't look ___!"
32 No longer new
33 Coral creation
34 Ham's word
35 FDR's mom
39 Actress Joanne
40 Botches the birdie?
42 Nile reptile
43 Leave the path
45 Dole's home
46 Bridal paths
49 American buffalo
50 "___ Want to Walk Without You"
51 Chromosome parts
52 Actress Lee
53 Hot spot
54 See 57 Down
55 Earth sci.
56 Washer fuzz
57 With 54 Down, *Cagney & Lacey* star
60 Call-day link
61 ___ *Tac Dough*

49 KID STUFF

by Trip Payne

ACROSS

1 It's often filed
5 Hold at fault
10 Some
14 Farming word form
15 Company takebacks
16 Sgt. Friday's employer
17 Burn the surface of
18 "This is only __"
19 Greek consonants
20 Kids' activity
23 Weaver sci-fi film
24 Sea shocker
25 Anderson's *High* __
27 Hwys.
28 Dutch cheese
32 G&S title character
34 Lawrence's locale
36 Actor Baldwin
37 Kids' activity
41 Ashbrook of *Twin Peaks*
42 Bulls, at times
43 Come out
46 Droops down
47 Promgoers: Abbr.
50 Outdated discs
51 College major
53 Actor Milo
55 Kids' activity
60 Right-hand person
61 Furnace fodder
62 One chip, often
63 Ship's staff
64 *Fiddler on the Roof* star
65 Hwys.
66 Turner and Danson
67 Huge number
68 Legal wrong

DOWN

1 Auto-racing org.
2 From time immemorial
3 Rafsanjani's followers
4 Greene of *Bonanza*
5 Bric-a-__
6 Riga resident
7 In __ (peeved)
8 General Dayan
9 High regard
10 Kal Kan competitor
11 Con man's specialty
12 Serial parts
13 Dict. entries
21 January, to Juan
22 Flavius' 551
26 Mythical bird
29 __ es Salaam
30 ". . . __ fat hen"
31 Cretan king
33 *Get Smart* baddies
34 Controversial tree spray
35 Taj Mahal city
37 Wiener-roast spot
38 Unbalanced
39 Canine command
40 Mr. Welles
41 Wilm.'s state
44 One-liner
45 Puts up a building
47 Japanese religion
48 Leaseholder
49 Most worldly-wise
52 Scout group
54 Maze word
56 11:00 feature
57 Hemingway's nickname
58 Plenty
59 Capri, for one
60 Make a decision

50 CAR-NATION

by Wayne R. Williams

ACROSS

1 Nightwear
8 Left undone
15 Admire a lot
16 Cane cutter
17 Silverdome home
19 *Gorillas in the Mist* director
20 Visitor from space
21 Rating unit
22 Free-for-all
24 Mini-army
28 Self-satisfied
30 Vacation spot
32 __ Baba
35 Rachins of *L.A. Law*
37 Eagle's nest
38 W.J. Bryan's home
42 Furnishings
43 Architect of St. Paul's
44 Slippery catch
45 Common mushroom
47 Like some Fr. nouns
49 Meeting: Abbr.
50 Mad. Ave. guy
53 Virginia dance
57 Moffo and Magnani
59 Desert Storm target
60 Marshal Dillon's home
65 Adds territory
66 Most creepy
67 Not at all polite
68 Power et al.

DOWN

1 __ *Delicate Condition* ('63 film)
2 Take up
3 Ruling group
4 Lets out, maybe
5 __ Marian
6 One-time connection
7 Wine word
8 Funt's request
9 More like a fine fabric
10 Rue one's run
11 Arm of the Pacific
12 Beer barrel
13 Schedule abbr.
14 Retreat
18 __ de mer
22 Comic Martin
23 First governor of Alaska
25 Mythology branch
26 Toddler's transportation
27 Big bargain
29 Native New Zealander
31 Has coming
32 Robert and Alan
33 Hamlet, to Horatio
34 Ancient Peruvians
36 Dir. opp. SSE
39 Formal flowers
40 Columnist Bombeck
41 High-fiber food
46 Stamp a stamp
48 Head-y word form
51 Henry James' __ *Miller*
52 CO clock setting
54 Ruhr Valley city
55 Wipe clean
56 Holds up
58 Waiting-room call
59 Roseanne, originally __
60 Bit of butter
61 Top ranking
62 Genetics letters
63 To date
64 Cipher code

51 FIRST LADIES?

by Mel Rosen

ACROSS

1 VHS alternative
5 Hens or mares
9 Not quite closed
13 Cheer words
14 Packs down
16 Path or phone opener
17 Satan's doings
18 ___ asst. (office aide)
19 "You're So ___" (Simon song)
20 Comic actress
23 Ping-Pong need
24 Common Mkt. money
25 Big-beaked birds
27 Conducts (oneself)
32 Ski lift
33 Lawyers' org.
34 Reaches quick conclusions
36 ___ nous
39 Civil case
41 Hogan rival
43 Revue, e.g.
44 *One Touch of ___*
46 Wish granter
48 Put to work
49 Finished a cake
51 States
53 Makes minor adjustments
56 Decimal base
57 "What ___ doing?"
58 *Charlie's Angels* actress
64 Skirt length
66 *Glengarry Glen Ross* playwright
67 Soil additive
68 Psyche sections
69 Nimble-legged
70 New Haven students
71 Make a bad impression
72 Building wings
73 Two-year-olds

DOWN

1 *Song of the South* title
2 Chalet overhang
3 Rarefied
4 Out like a light
5 Heights
6 "If I ___ Hammer"
7 Small-screen award
8 Like some milk
9 Off-road transport, in short
10 *Shane* star
11 Martian, e.g.
12 Leases out
15 Snobbish type
21 EPA concern
22 Cartoonist Goldberg
26 Preserves, in a way
27 HBO's system
28 Bassoon's relative
29 Audrey Hepburn's singing stand-in
30 Sharp taste
31 Ten-___ bicycle
35 Sensible
37 Mrs. Kennedy
38 Woolly beasts
40 Nip's partner
42 Gives orders
45 Go after
47 TVA product
50 Stage production
52 Bobby-sock relative
53 Brought under control
54 Mental picture
55 Rocket section
59 Actor Jannings
60 Congeal
61 Grain building
62 Skip over
63 Capone's nemesis
65 -arian relative

52 AMAZING PHRASING

by Wayne R. Williams

ACROSS

1 Dawber or Shriver
4 *Exodus* author
8 Removed soap
14 Southern st.
15 Window glass
16 Main course
17 Flap one's gums
18 Goodman's nickname
20 Before, poetically
21 *Xanadu* rock group
22 Narrow opening
23 Overact
25 In force
27 Make one
30 Ali technique
32 Altar words
33 Flows out
35 Greek letter
36 Beatle in the background
38 Sheet fabric
40 Soil
42 Earn after taxes
43 Eur. nation
44 Chocolate products
45 Pay stub?
46 Charity race
50 Tongue-clicking sound
51 Classic sagas
52 "I Am Woman" singer
55 Prof.'s rank
56 __ chi (martial art)
58 Anonymous John
59 Meet requirements
63 Quaint hotel
64 Excessively affected
65 Like Nash's lama
66 "Ready or __, here I come!"
67 Lyndon's running mate
68 Important times
69 Important time

DOWN

1 Check name
2 Cause anxiety
3 Be critical
4 Maintenance cost
5 Support bar
6 Do something new
7 Portion: Abbr.
8 Toss another coin
9 Ones in the know
10 Product package info.
11 __ Lanka
12 Poet's dusk
13 BA or MBA
19 Cold capital
24 Puccini opera
26 Nabokov novel
27 Entertain lavishly
28 Bergen or Buchanan
29 Cabinet features
31 Cave-dwelling fish
33 Florida attraction
34 Hour indicators
37 Permeate
39 Cop, at times
40 Giving a leg up to
41 Go wrong
43 Super Bowl team's div.
47 Outcome
48 Marquee word
49 Superfluous items
53 Philanthropist
54 Overinquisitive one
55 Old one: Ger.
57 Nautical direction
59 Six ft., at sea
60 Debt letters
61 Seles shot
62 Long scarf

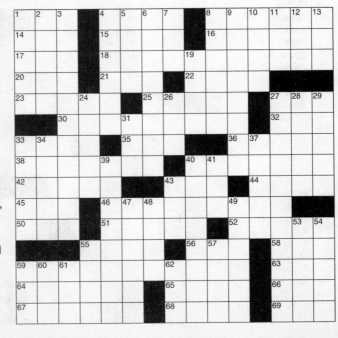

ACROSS

1 First vice president
6 Use a camcorder
10 *Born Free* roarer
14 Make a new wager
15 Astronaut Shepard
16 Follow behind
17 Quite clearly
20 __ distance (far away)
21 Comedienne Charlotte et al.
22 Where llamas roam
23 Musical breather
24 "__ but known!"
26 Is inconsistent
33 Bring down the house
34 Starchy side dish
35 Sticky stuff
36 Santa __, CA
37 Had hopes
40 Mr. Chaney
41 Headline of '14
42 Caviar versions
43 Laura of *Blue Velvet*
44 Total difference
49 Takes home
50 Oklahoma Indians
51 Reference book
54 Cartoonist Peter
55 *The Golden Girls* name
58 Completely
62 Make angry
63 Screenwriter James
64 Kind of kitchen
65 Milky gemstone
66 Forest growth
67 Room to maneuver

DOWN

1 Diva's solo
2 Fender bender
3 Eban of Israel
4 Blanc or Brooks
5 Takes a long look
6 Learn to like
7 "Too bad!"
8 Review poorly
9 Put a stop to
10 Kind of pride
11 __-back (relaxed)
12 Locale
13 Pub servings
18 Legal tender
19 In a clump
23 "Concord Hymn" monogram
24 Hide's partner
25 Suffix for attend
26 Rowdy to-do
27 Polynesian porch
28 Arkansas range
29 Actress Van Devere
30 Stared rudely
31 "Too-Ra-__-Loo-Ral"
32 Marie Osmond's brother
37 *Gunsmoke* star
38 "And __ goes"
39 Board inserts
43 Shingle letters
45 Nail polish
46 Rich cakes
47 __ time (never)
48 Rope loops
51 Oversized hairdo
52 Game-show prize
53 Entertainer Falana
54 Iowa city
55 Greek letter
56 Author Ambler
57 Diarist Frank
59 Scottish topper
60 Swelled head
61 Beer barrel poker?

54 NEW WORDS

....

by Mel Rosen

ACROSS

1 Not fully shut
5 Track circuits
9 Evert of tennis
14 Mexican nosh
15 Give off
16 Port-au-Prince's land
17 Musical work
18 Meatless patty
20 Back of the neck
21 USNA grad
22 Put away
23 Infuriated
25 Plaster paintings
29 LAX stats
30 Little bits
31 Away from the office
32 Soda buys
34 Sidekick
35 Colorado Indian
36 Hirt and Pacino
37 Like Cajun food
40 Computer screen: Abbr.
41 Winter bug
42 Big cheeses
43 Barbecue leftovers?
45 Musical discernment
46 Reminiscent of port
47 Get ready, for short
48 The whole shootin' match
50 Signify
53 Business abbr.
54 "My __ Sal"
55 Surmounting

56 Jet-setters
60 Roll on the tarmac
61 Nick of *48 HRS.*
62 "__ a man with seven wives"
63 Ear-related
64 Lost color
65 Cut back
66 Mythical birds

DOWN

1 Make up (for)
2 Honshu's land
3 Massage method
4 Optimistic
5 Protective embankments
6 Make a change to

7 Pen pals?
8 Relig. title
9 Mail channels
10 Rabbit's cousins
11 Predetermine the outcome
12 Mineral suffix
13 Military address
19 Figaro's job
24 Huff and puff
25 Loses color
26 TV addict
27 Bizarre
28 Leaves in the manuscript
30 A little weird
32 Sidewalk eateries

33 God of Islam
34 Impressionist's work
38 Show plainly
39 Tall tale
44 Hill figure
46 On a poster, perhaps
47 Nice to deal with
49 Please, in Potsdam
50 Provide food (to)
51 Poisonous
52 Grand tales
54 Explorer Vasco da __
56 Econ. datum
57 Mauna __
58 Unsatisfactorily
59 Actor Torn

55 MUSIC LESSON

by Mel Rosen

ACROSS

1 Woolly beasts
5 __ Penh, Cambodia
10 Prefix for light
13 Newspaper section, for short
14 Residence
15 Span. ladies
16 Musical embellishments
18 Break the news
19 Kind of kick
20 Worth salvaging
22 Bradley and Sullivan
23 Light into
24 Good relations
27 "His Master's Voice" co.
28 Say "howdy" to
31 Say it isn't so
32 Paper Mate rival
33 Brawn
34 Dict. abbr.
35 Musical conclusion
37 Perjure oneself
38 Whom Simple Simon met
40 Actor Beatty
41 Ponce de __
42 Seer's deck
43 Off-rd. transportation
44 Portsider's nickname
45 Glove leathers
47 Battery size
48 Swizzle stick
50 Eccentric senior
54 Roger Rabbit, for one
55 Ultra-loud, musically
58 Jillian and Sothern
59 Receded
60 Kimono closers
61 Roll-call response
62 Bridle straps
63 After-tax amounts

DOWN

1 Therefore
2 Put on
3 Greek letters
4 It may be high
5 Window glass
6 Cable channel
7 *Wayne's World* catchword
8 Black Sea port
9 Western hills
10 Musical symbol
11 Berlin had one
12 Seagirt land
15 Cellar access
17 Nelson of old films
21 Not specific
23 Musical stresses
24 Keep up with the times
25 __ event (photo op)
26 Chord transpositions
27 Free (of)
29 *Silas Marner* author
30 Smaller than small
32 Throw out
33 1400, in old Rome
35 Supply food for
36 Calif. neighbor
39 Bewails
41 Entices teasingly
43 Kind of bacterium
44 Southeast Asian land
46 Put aside
47 Etching liquids
48 Stand pat
49 Musical sound
51 Taunt
52 Give off
53 "It's My Turn" singer
56 Slugger's stat.
57 Perfect score, often

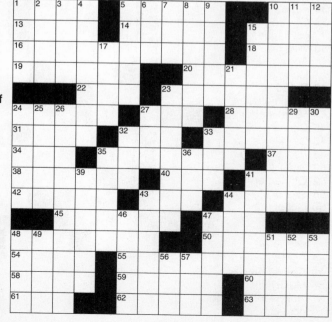

56 SIMPLE FARE

by Wayne R. Williams

ACROSS

1 Health haven
4 Barn baby
9 Call up
14 Floral loop
15 String-quartet member
16 Ancient Greek region
17 Simple, foodwise?
19 Put into effect
20 __ Stanley Gardner
21 Asian celebration
22 Movie parts
23 Satisfy
25 To be, in Toulouse
27 Polite word
28 Catcallers' compatriots
33 CIA forerunner
36 Pope's crown
39 Che's colleague
40 With 64 Across, simple, foodwise?
43 Noted violinmaker
44 Mural starter
45 Citrine quaff
46 Stocking style
48 Pedigree org.
50 Small fly
52 Of the nerves
56 *War of the __*
60 Out of the ordinary
62 Singer McEntire
63 Parting word
64 See 40 Across
66 Municipal
67 Hollywood's golden boy?
68 Poor grade
69 Move furtively
70 Good-guy group
71 Isr. neighbor

DOWN

1 Nod off
2 Irritation creation
3 Congregation separation
4 Eggs: Lat.
5 Climbing shrub
6 Easy gait
7 Privileged few
8 Inventor's initials
9 Something simple, foodwise?
10 Sharpen
11 __ even keel
12 Riviera resort
13 Breaks a fast
18 Some votes
22 Sellout sign
24 Something simple, foodwise?
26 Waldheim's predecessor
29 Aunt, in Alicante
30 Novelist Ferber
31 Funny Foxx
32 Roy Rogers' real name
33 Norwegian king
34 __ Valley, CA
35 Jamaican tunes
37 Japanese dog
38 __ Tin Tin
41 Ordinal ending
42 Some doters
47 USN rank
49 Street edge
51 Sort of sculpture
53 Studies
54 Historic Dublin theatre
55 Hen, for one
56 Fem. soldiers
57 Valhalla VIP
58 Bank of France?
59 *Star Wars* princess
61 Medicos
64 Vain man
65 "You __ what you eat"

57 POWER PLAY

by Mel Rosen

ACROSS

1 Raced Mark Spitz
5 "__ Ha'i"
9 F-sharp's alias
14 __'-shanter
15 Puts to work
16 Green hue
17 Abbr. in Bartlett's
18 Clock face
19 Judge's prop
20 Powerful, in the weight room
23 Musical transition
24 Comic Philips
25 Work with acid
29 Not for
31 Do cobbling
33 West of *Batman*
36 DeLuise film of '80
39 Underwater shocker
40 Powerful, in business
44 Eur. nation
45 Stratum
46 Aware of
47 Business-page listings
49 Stable baby
52 Twelve Oaks neighbor
53 Get __ for effort
56 Hallow
59 Powerful, in a crisis
63 1492 vessel
66 Cabbagelike plant
67 Jai __
68 Quite mature
69 __ on (goads)
70 Kindergarten breaks
71 Is overfond
72 Vast amounts
73 Three, in Toledo

DOWN

1 RR terminals
2 Wish-list items
3 Love, Italian-style
4 Marital fidelity
5 Spending plan
6 Laos' locale
7 Tenant's pact
8 Mideast belief
9 Full of energy
10 Linen plants
11 Actress Ullmann
12 Rosary prayer
13 __ Aviv
21 Convent dweller
22 Scandinavian
26 Wheel-alignment term
27 Soccer-shoe feature
28 Conversation starter
30 Not certain
32 Very long time
33 Sailor's shout
34 River region
35 __ Day (tree-planting time)
37 Tankard filler
38 Surf partner
41 Sort
42 Nose-related
43 Open-minded
48 Big house
50 Preoccupy
51 Chicken __ king
54 Reeboks' rivals
55 Old truism
57 Kind of power
58 Land or sea ending
60 Bran source
61 Aquatic organism
62 Show of affection
63 Paper tablet
64 Oath words
65 Fanatic follower

58 STATELY SOLVING

·······························

by Trip Payne

ACROSS

1. *Hill Street Blues* actress
6. Health hangout
9. 4/1 victims
14. Out of the way
15. Some votes
16. Parks and Bonheur
17. What "they call the wind"
18. Capp and Capone
19. North's nickname
20. Washington's state gem
23. Maryland's state sport
24. Plant part
28. Stay in hiding
32. Cockpit person
33. Started the hand
36. Hardwood tree
37. Abba of Israel
38. Modine movie of '84
39. *To Live and Die __*
40. Free (of)
41. Actor Willie
42. Slow mover
43. Dinkins and Bradley
45. Pom or pug
46. Wisconsin's state domestic animal
50. Alaska's state fossil
55. Two-faced god
56. Tread the boards
57. 24-book poem
59. "Not on __!" ("Never!")
60. Highlands refusal
61. Slow tempo
62. High-IQ group
63. Snake's sound
64. Misplaces

DOWN

1. Amateur-radio operator
2. Memo abbr.
3. Swampland
4. Revise copy
5. Corporate plane
6. Messed-up situation
7. Greek city-state
8. Good quality
9. Show disapproval of
10. Bird's-egg study
11. Chilly capital
12. Installed carpeting
13. Vane dir.
21. Charged atom
22. Lalapalooza
24. With 31 Down, Connecticut's state animal
25. Leg bone
26. "Luck Be __"
27. Calendar abbr.
29. Pearl City porch
30. Country singer K.T. __
31. See 24 Down
33. Not well-lit
34. Palindromic preposition
35. Paid notices
38. Pesto ingredient
39. Lodging place
41. Asian inland waterway
42. Lumber center
44. Aromas, in Exeter
45. Part of FCC
47. __ *Hope* (old soap)
48. Workout places
49. Actress Phoebe
50. Step through water
51. __ even keel
52. Muffin spread
53. Some containers
54. Can't stand
55. Freeway snarl
58. __ and don'ts

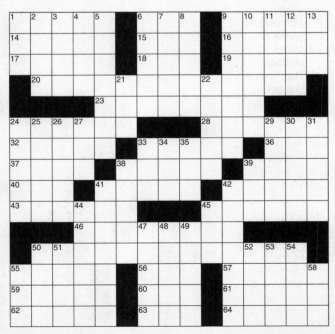

59 CULT CARTOON

by Mel Rosen

ACROSS

1 Fast-food drink
5 Proficient
9 Mr. Kadiddle-hopper
13 Wading bird
14 Grande and Bravo
15 Give up
16 Flying cartoon hero
19 Wide shoe width
20 Something funny
21 React to a pun
22 Place
23 Come up short
24 Destructive one
27 Eat well
28 Undergrad degs.
31 Make a complaint
32 Varieties
33 Bonn exclamation
34 Spy foes of 16 Across
38 Compass pt.
39 Dairy-case buys
40 Tall grass
41 Alert color
42 Feels bad about
43 Adjective for Merman
45 Rifles and revolvers
46 Appear to be
47 Maestro's stick
49 Psychic's sight
50 Work to do
53 Best friend of 16 Across
56 Territories
57 Jazz phrase
58 Castaway's home
59 Circle segments
60 Med-school subj.
61 Author Uris

DOWN

1 Become a father
2 Bassoon's kin
3 Monopoly props
4 Seek knowledge
5 More Bohemian
6 Old theater name
7 At sea
8 Atty.'s title
9 Yuletide music
10 Milan money
11 Equally balanced
12 Singer Tormé
15 Most lean and strong
17 Buffalo's lake
18 Kampala's country
22 Burt Reynolds' ex
23 Helsinki natives
24 Earth tone
25 Rope loop
26 Took a chance
27 Foolish capers
28 Diamond sacks
29 Dull pains
30 Not really legit
32 Pants parts
35 Misfortunes
36 Reunion invitees
37 Composer Khachaturian
43 Deprived (of)
44 Paper measure
45 Man of the world?
46 Bacteria fighter
47 Jefferson's VP
48 Actor Baldwin
49 Related
50 San __, CA
51 European capital
52 "I've __ had!"
53 Cote comment
54 New Deal agcy.
55 Tin Man's need

60 FRUCTIFEROUS

by Bob Lubbers

ACROSS

1. Rat-__
5. Break off
9. Uses a VCR
14. Solemn ceremony
15. *La __ aux Folles*
16. Without __ (broke)
17. Kemo __ (Tonto's pal)
18. Waikiki wiggle
19. Rent document
20. Tea variety
23. Tea holder
24. Singer Cole
25. Creeps along
27. Chew the fat
28. The __ the earth (kindly one)
30. Made a stack
33. Mrs. Roy Rogers
34. Big brass
37. Actress Meyers
38. Half a ten-spot
39. Buddhist sect
40. __ Cass Elliot
42. Peggy and Pinky
43. Nodded off
45. Marsh birds
47. Cratchit's kid
48. Heavenly lights
50. DC landmark
54. Bordeaux buddy
55. Clam variety
58. __ Carta
60. *Hud* Oscar winner
61. Three of a kind
62. Vermonter Allen

63. "__ each life . . ."
64. British prep school
65. Supple
66. Active one
67. Family rooms

DOWN

1. Fiery ambition?
2. Royal crown
3. Facing the pitcher
4. __ *Mutant Ninja Turtles*
5. Earl of car-painting fame
6. Brown shade
7. Give the eye
8. Highest level
9. Scout's quest
10. Old pro
11. Adolescent's "beard"
12. Come next
13. Flights have them
21. Pleased
22. NFLer or NHLer
26. Army bed
28. Puts away
29. Pub supply
30. Robin's *Mork & Mindy* costar
31. Author Levin
32. Chaplin film of '52
33. Calorie-counter's concern
35. Nectar collector
36. "__ then I wrote . . ."
38. Pink shade
41. Heretofore
43. Sour-cream concoctions
44. Skipped over
46. Repair a chair
47. "You've Got a Friend" singer
48. Veronica of *Hill Street Blues*
49. Fine fiddle
50. Rickety auto
51. Rich cake
52. Burger topping
53. Spinks and Uris
56. Oklahoma city
57. Betting setting
59. Slangy refusal

61 PRECISELY!

by Mel Rosen

ACROSS

1 Was an agent
6 Daytime TV fare
11 Three, in Turin
14 Like a washing-machine filter
15 Part of a ream
16 Free (of)
17 Precise, as to facts
19 Half of bi-
20 Day laborer
21 ___ in "apple"
22 Most up-to-date
24 "What's ___ for me?"
26 Take turns
27 Jazz fan
30 Paid escort
31 Cobbler's tool
32 Rose portion
34 Multi-person race
37 Teachers' grp.
38 Evans and Robertson
40 "___ Got Sixpence"
41 Practice routine
44 Ziti or rigatoni
46 Five-spot
47 ___ *Off* (Burnett film)
49 Implants
51 Soda-shop order
52 Johnson of *Laugh-In*
53 Mecca pilgrim
54 Mao ___-tung
55 Close loudly
59 Like Methuselah

60 Precise, as to appointments
63 ___ glance (quickly)
64 Nintendo forerunner
65 Easy victories
66 Poodle size
67 Madagascar mammal
68 Flooded with water

DOWN

1 Feed the pigs
2 Maine's state tree
3 Enthusiastic about
4 Kind of pride or food
5 Use henna
6 Short and wide
7 Inning's sextet
8 River islet
9 Play intro
10 State representative
11 Precise, in painting
12 Car-wash step
13 Use a blue pencil
18 Set a trap
23 It may be tall
25 Short snooze
26 Gets one's goat
27 Poker holding
28 Vase-shaped pitcher
29 Precise, in speaking
30 Festive events

33 Patched, perhaps
35 Rarin' to go
36 Hankerings
39 Hi-fi system
42 Lounge about
43 Not exaggerated
45 Tsp. or tbsp.
48 Middle Easterner
50 Give a gift
51 Very, in music
52 Up and about
53 Castle adjunct
54 Finished, for short
56 Peru's capital
57 Audio boosters
58 Fit together
61 School of whales
62 Gun org.

by Trip Payne

ACROSS

1 Fergie's first name
6 Sudden sound
10 Lie in the sun
14 Uneven
15 MP's quest
16 Not fooled by
17 Sprang up
18 Give an assessment
19 Singer Redding
20 Aliens, supposedly
23 Second person
24 Crossed out
25 Grammarian's concern
27 Baggage handlers
30 Play a part
32 Golf prop
33 Hearty brew
34 What some play by
35 Sharp pull
36 Alien vehicles
40 *Get Smart* group
41 Drain, as energy
42 Actress Caldwell
43 Quite cold
44 Author Du Bois
45 Goulash spice
49 Gettysburg general
51 Assistance
52 The bottom line
53 Meeting with an alien
58 Household helper
59 Sharp pull
60 TV exec Arledge

61 Words of approximation
62 Cleveland's lake
63 Loudness units
64 Banned pesticides
65 Husky's burden
66 Concerning

DOWN

1 Paint coat
2 Get in
3 Showed team spirit
4 Helper: Abbr.
5 Ladder base
6 Trash boats
7 Bestow
8 Mini-missive
9 High-spiritedness
10 Ship poles
11 Picnicker's pet?
12 Brandy cocktails
13 Boxing stats
21 Outlay
22 Eccentric type
26 Squealing shout
28 Low islands
29 __ Baba
30 They go tow-to-tow: Abbr.
31 Brazilian money
34 Mentalist's claim
35 Scoff at
36 King, but not prince
37 Spanish Civil War fighter
38 Chatter
39 *Beverly Hills* __
40 Kipling novel
44 Director Craven
45 Settled on
46 Chant
47 Actor __ Ivory Wayans
48 Not moving
50 Extinct birds
51 Potts of *Designing Women*
54 "I Only Have __ for You"
55 Viscount's superior
56 Bear, to astronomers
57 *Darkness at* __
58 Stylish, for short

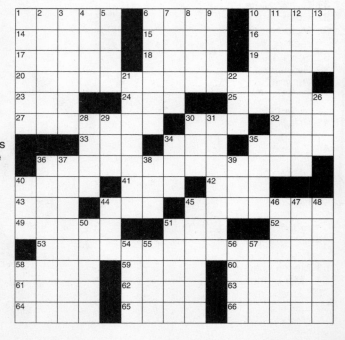

63 AMENDMENTS

by Shirley Soloway

ACROSS

1 Reach across
5 Mardi __
9 Free rides
14 Angel topper
15 Make a scene
16 Soaps actress Slezak
17 Scandinavian city
18 Sicilian spewer
19 Anglo-__
20 Transfer ownership
23 Compass pt.
24 Jay's follower
25 Top pilots
26 Funny Foxx
28 Done with
29 *Raging Bull* star
31 Anti-Dracula weapon
34 Winslow Homer painting
36 Ceramic square
37 Waker-upper
39 From Florence: Abbr.
40 Scared off
42 Bell sound
43 Alludes (to)
44 Sharp pain
46 Make over
47 Fizzy drink
48 Deli meat
51 British brew
53 Lighting accessory
56 Sired, old-style
58 Day's receipts
59 Olympian warmonger
60 __ Gay (WWII plane)
61 At any time
62 Nifty
63 Last-place finisher
64 Parcel (out)
65 Jane Austen novel

DOWN

1 Surprise, and then some
2 Turkish title
3 Calm down
4 Lunch time
5 Corfu's country
6 CBS anchorman
7 Christie and Karenina
8 Getz of jazz
9 Abates
10 Author Levin
11 Kind of mortgage
12 Ring decisions
13 Fully competent
21 Made a donation
22 Dorothy's Oz visit, e.g.
27 Processing veggies
28 '40s actor Dennis
29 __ *Rosen-kavalier*
30 Whitish gem
31 Part of MST
32 Wedding-cake level
33 Inseparable friends
34 Having the blues
35 Plumber's connection
37 Traffic-sign shape
38 Guitarist Paul
41 Soviet symbol
42 Prefix for sack
44 Shirt feature
45 Stick (to)
47 Barrel part
48 Sultan's pride
49 First-string players
50 *Call Me Madam* inspiration
51 Second son
52 Emcee Jay
54 Gossipy tidbit
55 Country road
57 Chilean cheer

64 DO SOMETHING!

by Trip Payne

ACROSS

1 Blessed events
7 Wax-coated cheese
11 Reb general Stuart
14 Third of an inning
15 Levee kin
16 Bunyan's tool
17 Olmos movie of '87
20 Paris airport
21 True-blue
22 Brewery hot spot
23 May honoree
24 Video room
25 He went east of Eden
27 Least dangerous
29 __ Monica, CA
33 Nepal native
36 Personal quirks
38 Campy exclamation
39 Become brave enough
42 Refrain bit
43 Martin Mull's *Roseanne* role
44 Donkey's comment
45 Work a puzzle
47 Depressed sorts
49 Not on the job
51 Fleur-de-__
52 Actor Kilmer
55 Not to mention
58 Mr. Doubleday
60 Tractor-trailer
61 Take up arms
64 Mamie's man
65 Blackjack cards
66 Eerie get-together

67 Marked out
68 Congressman Gingrich
69 Attacks

DOWN

1 __ buddies (close pals)
2 Preface, for short
3 Kingdom
4 Cereal tiger
5 Paul Newman role
6 Chess result
7 Sea swirl
8 Preachy, as literature
9 Scouting leader
10 Director Brooks
11 Coffee, so to speak
12 Former spouses
13 Ernie's roommate
18 Not a soul
19 New York college
24 Spotted, as a horse
26 Distributors
27 Capote's nickname
28 Person in a pool
30 Biblical sailor
31 Forum wear
32 Several
33 "Master" NCOs
34 Man of the hour
35 Bibliography abbr.

37 Estate sharer
40 Do-it-yourself beer
41 Scale notes
46 Shop clamp
48 First-year cadet
50 Joust weapon
52 Leaf channels
53 Chevron rival
54 Irish export
55 Grand __ racing
56 Delight in
57 Pre-owned
59 Hummingbird's home
60 Chair part
62 Ziering of *Beverly Hills 90210*
63 Golfer Trevino

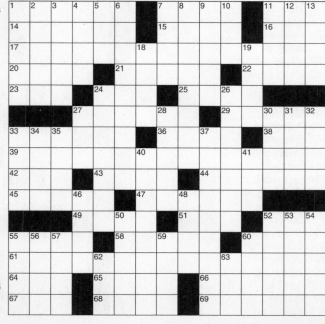

65 GETTING PHYSICAL

by Mel Rosen

ACROSS

1 One or the __
6 Historical period
9 Auction actions
13 Panda land
14 Wernher __ Braun
15 TV and radio
16 Carryalls
17 Catchall abbr.
18 Salad veggie
19 On the town
20 Start work, perhaps
23 Split __ (be too fussy)
25 Orchestra member
26 Onetime deliverers
28 Hee-haw
29 Airline to Tokyo
32 Bill on a cap
33 Venetian-blind part
34 Author Victor
35 Norwegian king
36 Brown shade
37 Parisian pals
38 Pasta alternative
39 Church area
40 Twofold
41 Asian ox
42 Picnic pests
43 Landlord's client
44 In the old days
45 20 percent
46 Child's song
50 Lodge member
53 Sandy's owner
54 Shout disapproval
55 Cosmic Carl
57 Adjust a lens
58 Easily deflated item
59 Piano piece
60 Student's hurdle
61 Free (of)
62 Closely packed

DOWN

1 Prefix meaning "eight"
2 Holier-than-__
3 Go to bed
4 Helmsman's dir.
5 More throaty
6 Makes level
7 Coll. army program
8 Alaska city
9 Uncle Miltie
10 Word form for "thought"
11 Platter
12 Can. province
15 Hatfield foe
21 Coffee maker
22 Ease up
24 Get __ on (rush)
26 Scrimshaw stuff
27 Eyelashes
28 Elated state
29 Make a false start
30 Quick on one's feet
31 Also-ran
33 Start to fall?
34 Visit often
36 Baccarat announcement
40 Did a bomb-squad job
42 Chips in
43 Carioca's home
44 Religion, to Karl Marx
45 Inundate
46 Sound's partner
47 Fort __, KY
48 Ancient Peruvian
49 Guru's title
51 Small boys
52 Patella's site
56 Had a bite

66 COUNTRY FOLKS

by Alex Vaughn

ACROSS
1 Finance degs.
5 Texas A&M rival
8 Leaves out
13 Utah resort
14 The census, e.g.
15 __ noir (red wine)
16 Betray boredom
17 Part of BTU
18 Lauder of lipsticks
19 Literature Nobelist in '21
22 Gets lost
23 FDR's dog
24 Vitamin quota: Abbr.
27 Old horse
29 Toddler swaddler
31 Witch
34 Boxer in the news
37 Plains natives
39 Easiness epitomized
40 Irene of *Fame*
41 *Life Wish* author
46 Ginza gelt
47 Seasoned veteran
48 Ms. Farrow
49 Aves. cross them
50 To be: Lat.
53 NL team
58 Basketball star
61 Miss something?
63 Insanity, at times
64 Painter Joan
65 Rocket brake

66 Cribbage need
67 Latch __ (get)
68 Quite pale
69 Mos. and mos.
70 Yawl pole

DOWN
1 Early Americans
2 He spoke for Daffy
3 Doing battle
4 December flier
5 Actor Franchot
6 *Cheers* character
7 Extremist
8 Out-of-doors
9 File category: Abbr.
10 Give-and-take
11 Sock part

12 Sault __ Marie, MI
14 Celestial object
20 Atlanta arena
21 *M*A*S*H* star
25 Plowman John
26 Indo-European
28 Stare open-mouthed
30 Pedigree org.
31 Orange-roof eatery, familiarly
32 Like Pisa's tower
33 Locket artisan
35 Zilch
36 Smile radiantly
38 VCR speed setting
42 Countrified affirmative

43 __ Hashanah
44 Kiddie turtle tetrad
45 Belafonte's holler
51 Over-sentimental
52 Fishing specialist
54 Keaton/Garr film of '83
55 Minneapolis suburb
56 Knave's booty
57 Stuck-up one
59 Legalese phrase
60 Chippendale quartet
61 Swimsuit part
62 Congressman Aspin

S-CAPADE

by Fred Piscop

ACROSS

1 Quasimodo creator
5 Pipemaker's material
8 Hiccup, e.g.
13 Right away: Abbr.
14 Raw metal
15 __ of the Jackal
16 THE STAR
18 Expose to the atmosphere
19 Commandment
20 Sitting room
21 Neighbor of Isr.
22 "We aim to __"
25 Cravings
26 __ Blow (average guy)
27 Hat material
29 __ spumante
32 Glum drop
34 Cronies
38 Cell, so to speak
40 Skilled worker
42 Hindu's destiny
43 __-de-camp
45 Tijuana nosh
46 Baker's need
48 "C'est la __!"
50 Prefix for space
53 Bird, often
55 Trophy shape
58 __ 17 ('53 film)
60 Alphabet inventor
62 "Could __ Magic" ('57 tune)
63 STAR'S LADY FRIEND
64 Close again
65 Tavern
66 Tehran's land
67 Charlie Chan portrayer
68 Wooden pin
69 __ out (supplements)

DOWN

1 Some fasteners
2 Loan-sharking
3 Sort of starer
4 Oil cartel
5 All-in-one
6 Speak on a soapbox
7 Mr. Jonson
8 Mets' stadium
9 STAR'S BOSS, AT TIMES
10 Allan-__
11 Squashed, maybe
12 Bristol's partner
15 Come to a point
17 Take-back, for short
23 Simile center
24 Valuable violin
26 STAR'S MALE FRIEND
28 Give a show
29 Pop a question
30 Hearst's kidnappers: Abbr.
31 Pavement material
33 Wipe out
35 UN member
36 Bub
37 __-cone (cool treat)
39 Ginnie __
41 Respecting deeply
44 "For what __ worth . . ."
47 Play backer
49 Some nest eggs: Abbr.
50 National Leaguer
51 Mrs. Mertz
52 Mrs. Gorbachev
54 Steak order
55 Lewis' partner
56 Forearm bones
57 Hammer parts
59 "I'm __ boy!" (Costello)
61 Nastase of tennis
63 Back talk

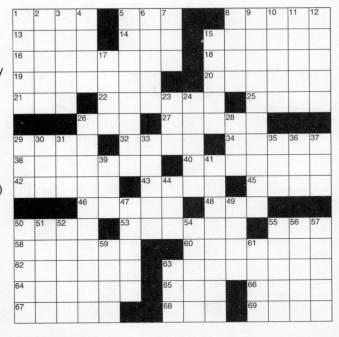

68 SPORTSMANSHIP

by Shirley Soloway

ACROSS

1 Cotton fabric
5 Yard tool
9 "So be it!"
13 Gusto
14 Preceding nights
15 St. Kitts-__ (Caribbean nation)
17 Takes chances on the rink?
20 Beret relative
21 Bordeaux et Champagne
22 Lucky charm
23 Drapery support
24 Singing sound
25 Start a swan dive?
32 Cool spot
34 Day saver
35 Piano piece
36 Helen's abductor
37 Prior to, in poetry
38 Furry fish-eater
39 Cupid's equivalent
40 Inflated psyches
41 Loud shouts
42 About to score on serve?
45 Pigpen
46 Days of yore
47 Mortar mate
51 __ cost (free)
53 Copacabana city
56 Getting close, in a race?
59 Vacancy sign
60 Beloved
61 Prince of opera
62 __ and Lovers
63 "__ forgive those . . ."
64 Actress Rowlands

DOWN

1 Pain in the neck
2 Chase of films
3 Polite address
4 Aardvark tidbit
5 Call home
6 Stratford's river
7 Teen dolls
8 Cleve.'s zone
9 Barbarian
10 Bistro list
11 Morally wrong
12 Riviera resort
16 Stuck in place
18 Calls forth
19 Silent screen star?
23 Salad veggie
24 Singer Brewer
25 Clairvoyant's card
26 Zorro, __ Blade
27 Crane's cousin
28 Never walked on
29 "__ I can help it!"
30 Cheerfulness
31 What walls may have
32 Shoot forth
33 Mata __
38 It's spotted in the zoo
40 Make an appearance
43 Cartographer's dots
44 London hub?
47 Dutch oven, e.g.
48 Genesis man
49 Normandy town
50 Afterwards
51 A long time
52 Spring event
53 Intense anger
54 Sect's symbol
55 Gumbo ingredient
57 Wyo. neighbor
58 Nautical gear

FRUIT SALAD

by Mel Rosen

ACROSS

1 Iceberg part
4 "Sink" or "swim"
8 Ranks high
13 Pisa dough
14 Roundish
15 Wear away
16 "What's the big __?"
17 *Doctor Zhivago* heroine
18 Mongol invader
19 Not fem.
20 Loud firecracker
22 Gibson of tennis
24 Gather in
25 Big jerk
27 Masters, for one
32 Office areas
37 Sketched out
38 Skin-cream additive
39 Sprinter's must
41 Made an unreturned serve
42 Sweeps upward
44 Harvesting machines
46 Complained
48 Fairway warning
49 Camp beds
52 Behind-the-scenes
56 "Nonsense!"
61 "Would __ to you?"
62 Told the world
63 Present time?

64 Church area
65 Crème de la crème
66 Treat meat
67 Greek letters
68 Houston's home
69 Makes a choice
70 Choose: Abbr.

DOWN

1 Kind of wave
2 "__ my case"
3 "Dandy!"
4 Pinatubo and Krakatoa
5 "Well, Did You __!" (Porter tune)
6 Less common
7 Loud sound

8 Did a letter over
9 Bedouin
10 Oz visitor
11 Dutch cheese
12 Belgrade native
13 Succotash bean
21 Teen's exclamation
23 Dumbo's wing
26 Keystone __
28 Info sources
29 Dash or relay
30 Water pitcher
31 Some footballers
32 On the toasty side
33 Mixed bag

34 Sub __ (secretly)
35 Came upon
36 Feudal worker
40 Bishops' districts
43 Withdraws (from)
45 Big leaguer
47 Big parties
50 Mexican resort
51 Provide a recap
53 Tickle pink
54 Be a match for
55 Some shirts
56 Aid in crime
57 Lose color
58 __-fixe menu
59 "__ smile be your umbrella . . ."
60 Tea table

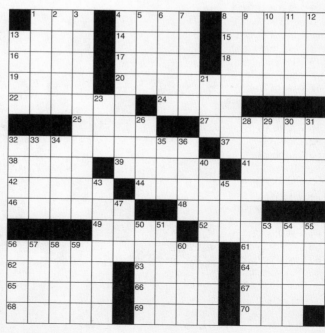

by Eric Albert

ACROSS

1 Mensa qualifier
7 Boy Scout's reference
15 Swain
16 Open to discussion
17 Western hero
19 "___ Smile Be Your Umbrella"
20 Boffo show
21 "No ___, ands, or buts!"
24 Brit's greeting
26 Lose brightness
30 Dust-jacket text
33 Frolicsome
34 Grandchild of Adam
35 Governmental system
37 Gizmo
39 Square-dance song
41 Sort of sword
43 Turn into steam
46 "Famous" cookiemaker
47 Actor Cariou
48 Artist's A-frame
49 Ancient story
50 Andrea ___
52 Clothes line
53 Cranberries' place
54 PDQ relative
57 Whoopi Goldberg film of '86
65 Silk headgear
66 Wears away
67 Wearying
68 Squirrel, for one

DOWN

1 Mr. Kabibble
2 Status ___
3 Inside info
4 List-ending abbr.
5 Where the rubber meets the road
6 Faithfulness
7 Old witch
8 In a mischievous manner
9 Mystery writer Marsh
10 Wipe the woodwork
11 ___-relief
12 Japanese sash
13 Of long standing
14 Important
18 Nothing at all
21 Apple rival
22 Andy Capp's wife
23 Astronomer's sighting
25 Pilot's break
26 It's often felt
27 Great suffering
28 Deer's daughter
29 Superlative suffix
31 Debonair
32 French cheese
36 EMT specialty
37 Rip off
38 Spiny succulent
40 Zealous sort
41 Wool source
42 A Little Woman
44 Last letter
45 Shade source
47 Big blockage
50 "Tiny Bubbles" singer
51 One with a query
53 Slant
55 Oversized hairdo
56 Walk wearily
57 Make a note
58 Wire-service abbr.
59 Mal de ___
60 Prefix for fix
61 Corroded
62 Citrus drink
63 State rep.
64 FDR's successor

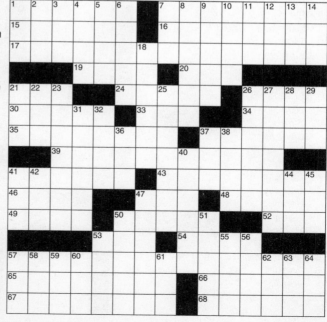

COMPARISONS

by Mel Rosen

ACROSS

1 Practice boxing
5 Break up
9 Work out on ice
14 Wash up
15 Bassoon relative
16 Heaps up
17 Voice of America org.
18 Wildcat
19 Showy display
20 Quick-witted
23 Plane holders
24 Datsun, nowadays
28 AP rival
29 New York stadium
31 Cable choice
32 Sagacious
36 Sounds of delight
37 Oath words
38 Sun. speech
39 Seafood delicacy
40 Bro or sis
41 Unfettered
46 "Annabel Lee" author
47 Hitchcock's __ *Window*
48 Cutesy suffix
49 Wimpole or Wall
51 Sponsors of a sort
55 Really irate
58 Have a nosh
61 Solitary
62 Tibetan monk
63 Blender setting
64 Rom. Cath. official
65 Estrada of *CHiPs*
66 Fed the kitty
67 Bean plants
68 Be worthy of

DOWN

1 Semi-melted snow
2 Turkish title
3 Bird-related
4 Debate again
5 The North Star
6 Chasm
7 Writer Jaffe
8 Schoolbook
9 Short-term sale
10 Soccer shots
11 The whole nine yards
12 1773 jetsam
13 Part of i.e.
21 "__ Doc" Duvalier
22 Over again
25 Puppeteer Lewis
26 Dislike a lot
27 __ around (snooped)
29 Scornful look
30 Israeli dance
32 Filmy strands
33 Dostoyevsky's *The __*
34 Levelheaded
35 On a cruise
41 __ out (went berserk)
42 On a pension: Abbr.
43 Volcanoes, e.g.
44 Top-notch
45 Soda maker
50 Variety-show host
51 Mean and low
52 Tara family name
53 Send money
54 Idaho river
56 Charity
57 Just fair
58 Hot tub
59 Convent resident
60 Mr. Buchwald

NAME-ING NAMES

by Eric Albert

ACROSS

1 Quite stylish
5 Wood-trimming tool
9 Monastery head
14 Late-night TV name
15 Make money
16 Zero people
17 Harsh, as weather
19 These times
20 BING
22 Choir offerings
23 Jimmy Carter's daughter
24 Sample soda
27 The night before
28 On edge
31 Jupiter's wife
32 Bring together
34 Civil-suit subjects
35 MING
40 Flatten
41 Up, on a map
42 State with confidence
43 Sir Newton
45 Shoot the breeze
48 Basinger of *Batman*
49 African snake
50 Delicate purple
52 RING
57 Man with a horn
59 Tropical fish
60 Basic belief
61 Stare stupidly
62 Dennis, to Mr. Wilson
63 Has in mind
64 *Born Free* character

65 Genealogy diagram

DOWN

1 Overused phrase
2 Shakespearean subject
3 What you earn
4 List-introducing punctuation
5 Peak
6 Person of action
7 Galvanization need
8 Catch, in a way
9 Champing at the bit
10 Hapless one
11 Ride the waves
12 "__ Clear Day"
13 Mystery writer Josephine
18 USN rank
21 "Peg __ Heart"
25 Excited by
26 Sit for shots
28 Lively dance
29 ET vehicle
30 Leading lady Loy
31 Kid around
32 Software runner
33 Gretzky's org.
34 Explosive initials
35 Hostile reaction
36 Jeans name
37 Common prayer

38 Film-noir classic
39 Mythical beast
43 Funnyman Kabibble
44 Sea creature
45 Author Grass
46 Not willing
47 Scold severely
49 Building blocks of matter
50 Gold-chained actor
51 Highly skilled
53 Familiar with
54 Honest-to-goodness
55 Nadirs
56 "My Way" singer
57 Rye partner
58 What a feller needs?

by Bob Lubbers

ACROSS

1 Short letter
5 No longer trendy
10 Did the butterfly
14 General Idi
15 Dangerous whales
16 Mexican money
17 Doris Day film of '59
19 Mr. Preminger
20 What you wear
21 Kenyan capital
23 Parking aide
25 Steel factory
26 Pasta shapes
28 Dwarf trees
31 Like __ of bricks
32 Rat-race result
34 FDR agency
35 Seamstress Ross
37 Corn unit
38 Accurate, pitchwise
40 Outs' partners
41 __ of Jeannie
44 Poetic nighttimes
45 Hats, so to speak
47 So far
49 Part to play
50 Pavarotti, for one
51 Elizabeth II's house
53 Beethoven opus
57 Author Morrison
58 Ductwork material
60 Suggest strongly
61 Floor, in France
62 Shaker contents
63 Porgy's love
64 Copter part
65 Normandy town

DOWN

1 Western wine region
2 Leave out
3 Pinball problem
4 Perks up
5 General Colin's family
6 Whistler works
7 Barely enough
8 Room, to Roberto
9 Kayak builders
10 Thread holders
11 Party pooper
12 Italy's answer to 1 Down
13 Pasture plaint
18 Evangelist Roberts
22 Duz rival
24 Organic compounds
26 Dictation taker
27 Arkansas resort
28 Chew out
29 Actress Dunne
30 Simon follower
31 Just slightly
33 *Norma* __
36 Investor's concern
39 Proximity
42 Bedroom piece
43 Godzilla or Rodan
46 Shetlands, e.g.
48 Unavoidable fate
50 Pick up the tab
51 Got tiresome
52 "__ be in England . . ."
54 Rat-__
55 Hard to believe
56 Palo __, CA
57 Rickety ship
59 Self-image

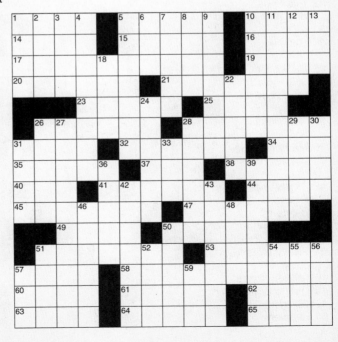

74 IT'S SHOW TIME!

by Eric Albert

ACROSS

1 Johann Sebastian __
5 Dick and Jane's dog
9 Son of Seth
13 .405 hectare
14 Knee-bone neighbor
16 Norway native
17 Jane Fonda film of '86
20 Chop down
21 Anti-flood structure
22 Senselessness
23 Beauteous group
24 Mr. Laurel
25 Sale sweetener
28 Smile broadly
29 Fast way to England
32 Eye-bending designs
33 All in
34 Concerned with
35 Pacino film of '75
38 Cools down, in a way
39 "Working or not"
40 Marry in haste
41 Bobby Orr's org.
42 Englishman, for short
43 Belmont Stakes winner in '75
44 Brought into being
45 Chicken fixin's
46 Girl, to Dundee
49 "Excuse me!"
50 Sundial's 7

53 Randy Quaid film of '78
56 *Exodus* author
57 Country singer Steve
58 Kind of vaccine
59 Nerd
60 African nation
61 Little shaver

DOWN

1 Shower alternative
2 Liniment target
3 Stagehands
4 Fabric border
5 Work hard
6 Little finger
7 Off-Broadway award
8 Soft metal
9 Like leprechauns
10 Post-WWII alliance
11 Cartel in the news
12 Energetic
15 Stir up
18 Folk-blues singer
19 Economist Smith
23 Epic poets
24 Does ushering
25 *The Thinker* sculptor
26 Noteworthy period
27 Roll with a hole
28 Are suited for
29 Snobby one
30 "His face could __ clock"
31 Copier need

33 Count of jazz
34 Bride's acquisition
36 Gridiron gain
37 Make over
42 It's east of Java
43 Karamazov brother
44 Capital of Belorussia
45 Nut case
46 Too confident
47 Take on
48 Singer Adams
49 Razor brand
50 Oft-used adverb
51 Meryl, in *Out of Africa*
52 Capri, for one
54 Swiss partner
55 Balderdash

GOOD SKATES

by Randolph Ross

ACROSS

1 Actress Gardner
4 Shipboard officers
9 TV host Donahue
13 Like a wet rag
15 Some exams
16 Not well-done
17 __ above (minimally)
18 '88 Olympics skater
20 Of a lord's estate
22 Beginning
23 '68 Olympics skater
26 Actor Alejandro
27 *Exodus* role
28 Mauna __
31 Grimm villain
34 Utmost, so to speak
36 '92 Olympics skater
40 Shares secrets
41 Converse
42 It's inspiring
43 Get __ of (eliminate)
44 Suns do it
46 '84 Olympics skater
52 Crazy as __
55 Paint solvents
56 '32 Olympics skater
59 Ms. Barrett
60 "Cheerio!"
61 *Look Back in __*
62 Tree knot
63 Haywire
64 Impolite looks
65 Els' followers

DOWN

1 ". . . __ unto my feet"
2 Curriculum __ (resumé)
3 In the company of
4 Make changes to
5 "And we'll have __ good time"
6 Postpone
7 Actor Wallach
8 Sleek plane
9 Fork tine
10 Deli meats
11 "Dies __" (hymn)
12 "__ we forget"
14 Go forward
19 Sharpening
21 Whiskey type
24 Address after "yes"
25 Film role for Shirley
28 Polish political name
29 Workplace agcy.
30 Working hard
31 Ark. neighbor
32 Got taller
33 Communion, e.g.
34 Marino or McGrew
35 Air carriers
37 Albania's capital
38 Monogram part: Abbr.
39 *The Empire Strikes Back* teacher
44 Shows contempt
45 Stop for a bite
46 Savalas role
47 Kitchen appliance
48 More frosty
49 Make a hole __
50 Midmorning
51 Peter and Nicholas
52 Nick Charles' pooch
53 Sandy soil
54 Familiar with
57 *2001* computer
58 Compass pt.

76 SO WHAT?

by Trip Payne

ACROSS

1 Barely open
5 Con game
9 Paper layers
14 US national flower
15 Balsa or balsam
16 Long gun
17 '77 Linda Ronstadt tune
19 Oil source
20 '84 Pointer Sisters tune
22 *Falcon Crest* star
26 Binge
27 Draft org.
28 Makes up (for)
30 Dolores __ Rio
32 Mrs. Truman
33 Cajun veggie
37 They hold water
40 '83 Lauper album
43 Kiss follow-up?
44 Piece of cake
45 Halves of quartets
47 Could possibly
49 Heavy-hitting hammer
51 Pedigree grp.
54 Snake poison
58 "__ my case"
59 '73 Carly Simon tune
62 Gourmand
63 '63 Chiffons tune
68 Skirt style
69 Midwestern tribe
70 Hertz rival
71 Gave a PG-13 to
72 Go down
73 College book

DOWN

1 Onassis, familiarly
2 Scribble (down)
3 Nincompoop
4 Musical notes
5 Wineglass part
6 Boorish and rude
7 Man with morals
8 Mr. Lansky
9 Goes forward
10 Caron movie
11 __ *Tuesday, This Must Be Belgium*
12 Arctic assistants
13 Burpee products
18 French river
21 Crossed out
22 Chemist's second home
23 Bomb tryout
24 General Dayan
25 11th-century saint
29 "Send help!"
31 Cosmetics name
34 Wins the bout
35 10-K, for one
36 Santa __ , CA
38 Bea Arthur sitcom
39 Walks heavily
41 Drooled
42 Pkg. co.
46 Matched group
48 "Without a doubt!"
50 Floor covering, for short
51 Once __ (annually)
52 Eucalyptus muncher
53 Make the grade
55 "Never!"
56 __ Culp Hobby
57 Bricklayer
60 Russo of *Lethal Weapon 3*
61 "Uh-huh . . ."
64 What *gras* means
65 "__ been had!"
66 Put the kibosh on
67 Guinness Book suffix

77 ORAL EXAM

by Bob Lubbers

ACROSS

1 Emerald Isle
5 "This is only __"
10 Open slightly
14 Author Vidal
15 Use pointlessly
16 Prohibition
17 Litter bit
19 Is in debt
20 Two-__ (small plane)
21 Show fear
23 Verdi work
26 Kuwaiti ruler
27 Cow quarters
30 Poem of praise
32 Pop singer Billy
35 Yale athletes
36 Mixed drink
38 In the past
39 Actress Ullmann
40 Leaf-covered
41 Josh around
42 Peggy or Pinky
43 European airline
44 Soccer great
45 Sign up
47 Dapper __
48 Peels off
49 Trumpet accessory
51 Not bogus
53 Stifle
56 Unfinished rooms
60 Serve tea
61 Just misses a putt
64 Caesarean phrase
65 Select group
66 Ms. McEntire
67 Attorney Roy
68 French painter
69 Sp. ladies

DOWN

1 Ham partners
2 Libertine
3 *My Friend __*
4 Isaac and Wayne
5 Cognizant (of)
6 Beer device
7 Mind reader's talent
8 Editor's notation
9 __ Haute, IN
10 Kind of energy
11 Very hard candy
12 Genesis son
13 Ploy
18 Agts., e.g.
22 Overdo a role
24 Stirred up
25 Nimitz's title
27 Ball girl?
28 Little green man
29 Delta's locale
31 Director May
33 Fast on one's feet
34 Junction points
36 Sailor, slangily
37 Greek letter
40 Dirty stuff
44 Talks quickly
46 Beat in a heat
48 Essential part
50 Fished, in a way
52 Fence openings
53 Chance-taking, for short
54 Lorre role
55 Make angry
57 Cake topper
58 Havana locale
59 Fitness centers
62 Pen dweller
63 RR stop

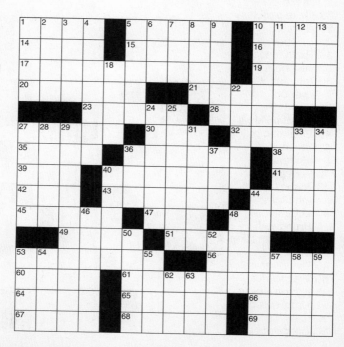

78 KID STUFF

by Eric Albert

ACROSS

1 Ralph __ Emerson
6 Lifeline locale
10 Wine barrel
14 Belted constellation
15 __ vera (shampoo ingredient)
16 Put money in
17 Kid-lit gold spinner
20 Leg joint
21 English prep school
22 Symbol of love
23 Vanquish a dragon
25 Potter's material
27 Squeezing snake
30 Make bubbles
31 Actress Dawber
34 Exclaimed in delight
35 Put something over on
36 Lucid
37 Kid-lit builders
40 Eccentric guy
41 St. Louis landmark
42 Fork parts
43 A question of method
44 Logan of Broadway
45 Sweet-smelling place
46 Dinner giver
47 Walesa, for one
48 __ von Bulow
51 Untrustworthy sort
53 Cluckers
57 Kid-lit siblings
60 Sty cry
61 Aroma
62 Copycat's phrase
63 The hunted
64 Actress Daly
65 Hurled

DOWN

1 Put in effort
2 Make __ for it
3 Jell-O flavor
4 Racetrack info
5 I, to Claudius
6 __-faced (pale)
7 Sax range
8 Tarzan's garment
9 Director Brooks
10 Deejay Kasem
11 "Diana" singer
12 Mix a martini
13 Superman's alter ego
18 Low in fat
19 Defrost
24 Mine find
26 Lounge lazily
27 Cover a hole
28 Exuberant cry
29 Lose on purpose
30 Make a mess of
31 *Common Sense* writer
32 Make mad
33 Needing cleaning
35 Mamie or Rosalynn
36 Shoe projection
38 Myanmar neighbor
39 Latin abbr.
44 "No way, __!"
45 Net star Bjorn
46 Sled dog
47 Army spiritual leader
48 Piece of pork
49 Den
50 Diarist Frank
52 Privy to
54 "__, Brute!"
55 Noble gas
56 Walk through mud
58 Unimproved land
59 Real-estate ad wd.

FIND AWAY

by Trip Payne

ACROSS

1 Mr. Selleck
4 Filibuster
9 Glove-box items
13 Gray's field: Abbr.
15 Poet Elinor
16 Kind of sax
17 Bethlehem trio
18 Sports stadium
19 Satiate
20 TV accessory
23 Start of a proverb about silence
24 Digger's tool
26 Rock singer John
27 Nicklaus' grp.
30 The other team
31 King of Norway
32 Swiss home
34 White alternative
35 Hippie's remark
38 White House nickname
41 Shopping sprees
42 Director Preminger
46 Fourbagger
48 Chariot suffix
49 Smug expression
50 Barbarian
52 Porcupine features
53 Midler top-10 tune of '90
57 Royal decree
58 *The Prince of Tides* star
59 Gobbles up
61 Comic Johnson

62 Perrier competitor
63 Organic compound
64 Have to have
65 "__ evil, hear . . ."
66 Secret stealer

DOWN

1 Scottish headgear
2 Continuously successful
3 Red shade
4 Sharp blows
5 Brit's radial
6 Actor Baldwin
7 Carpet alternative, for short
8 Relies (on)
9 Long-vowel indicator
10 Everywhere
11 Ancient astronomer
12 Sauce variety
14 Vacation period
21 Keep for oneself
22 Greek letter
23 New beginning?
25 Caustic chemical
27 Ring up
28 Measure
29 Raise the hem, maybe
32 Dernier __ (latest fashion)
33 Printer's measures

36 James __ Garfield
37 Possible award-winner
38 "What ho!"
39 Big blaze
40 Kuwait, for one
43 Soup holders
44 Lullaby locale
45 Signs off on
47 Hammed it up
49 Health resort
51 Bowling places
52 Office worker
54 Hawk's opposite
55 "Would __ to you?"
56 Ollie's pal
57 Ardent watcher
60 Foxlike

80 FICTIONAL PHYSICIANS

by Randolph Ross

ACROSS

1 Opera star Merrill
7 Prince Charles' sport
11 Wild blue yonder
14 Have __ many
15 Literary VIP
16 Hasten
17 MD once on ABC
19 Switch settings
20 Fruity dessert
21 Biblical twin
22 Illiterate endorser
24 Mlle. of Madrid
26 Combustible heaps
29 Recipe direction
32 *Star Trek* doctor
35 Send to cloud nine
36 Usually
37 Babysitter's banes
39 Memos
40 Scatterbrained sort
43 Gives testimony
45 MD once on NBC
47 Controversial tree spray
48 Thai or Mongol
49 Cub Scout units
53 Speedwagon maker
55 Starting
57 Mauna __
58 Oliver Stone film
60 Conan Doyle doctor
64 Pub order
65 Greek theaters
66 Chore
67 Future flower
68 Bastes or hems
69 Ear pollution

DOWN

1 Easy victories
2 TV studio sign
3 Artist's topper
4 List ender
5 No gentleman
6 Drunkard
7 Lung lining
8 Tulsa product
9 Slow pitch
10 Figurine mineral
11 Timesavers
12 Relatives
13 "You bet!"
18 *True Grit* Oscar-winner
23 Placed in a third-party account
25 *Compos mentis*
27 Chapter in history
28 '60s radical org.
30 Hercules' captive
31 Bakery buys
33 Lets up
34 Lord's land
35 Singled out
37 Mexican peninsula, for short
38 Irani money
41 Blotter initials
42 Insult, in current slang
43 "Add __ of salt . . ."
44 Dey's *L.A. Law* role
46 Forest vines
50 Lanchester et al.
51 All's opposite
52 Time, metaphorically
54 Eyes: Sp.
56 Old card game
58 Holyfield hit
59 Winter bug
61 Tribute in verse
62 Chop down
63 Pod prefix

81 STRIKE IT RICH

by Shirley Soloway

ACROSS

1 Beach surface
5 Western writer on a $5 stamp
10 Acting job
14 Small band
15 Factory group
16 Water pitcher
17 Part of CPA
18 Sober-minded
19 *Bus Stop* writer
20 Get rich quick
23 Button directive
24 After six
28 Grass purchase
29 Liza's Oscar film
33 Coral or Caribbean
34 Baseball exec Al
35 School grps.
36 Get rich quick
41 Cathedral area
42 Charlie Chan portrayer
43 British brew
44 Brain part
47 Señora Perón
50 Not at all friendly
52 Female fox
54 Get rich quick
58 A real clown
61 __ Boothe Luce
62 Environmental sci.
63 Genesis site
64 Floor installer
65 "Don't look __!"
66 Heredity unit
67 Derisive look
68 Church service

DOWN

1 Philatelist's fodder
2 Jockey Eddie
3 Cut a little
4 Is overfond of
5 Corn covering
6 Opposing one
7 Mideast money
8 Hard worker
9 Salad vegetable
10 Have sovereign power
11 __ up to (admit)
12 Turkey part
13 Prior to, in poems
21 Wide tie
22 Court barrier
25 Ratio phrase
26 Well-ordered
27 Regular, e.g.
30 Hardwood
31 Flying buzzer
32 Pear variety
34 Line on a map: Abbr.
35 Not COD
36 Saintly ring
37 Currier's partner
38 100 percent
39 White House nickname
40 Scoundrel
41 Slangy refusal
44 Russian space station
45 Votes in
46 Sell
47 Track bet
48 Some poisons
49 Bracelet holders
51 Steak order
53 Construction girder
55 Moolah
56 Nut source
57 Kohl's title
58 Canine command
59 Kind of poem
60 Buddhist sect

by Randolph Ross

ACROSS

1 Apply (to)
8 Keep at it
15 Hillary's height
16 Replenish inventory
17 Former *Today* cohost
19 Child pleaser
20 Oklahoma Indian
21 Els' followers
22 Mel of baseball
24 Gibbon, e.g.
25 Pitcher's stats
26 See 17-Across
31 Smith of Rhodesia
32 Green land
33 Fit for farming
37 Earned, so to speak
39 Frying pan
40 Lady of Spain
41 Oil acronym
42 "__ Clear Day"
43 *Today* semi-regular
46 African nation
49 Popular suffix
50 Some magazine pages
51 Ms. MacGraw
52 Levee kin
54 Leb. neighbor
56 *Today* cohost
62 Command stratum
63 Veal dish
64 Causing bias
65 Still standing

DOWN

1 Urban walker: Abbr.
2 Night before
3 Soldier in gray
4 TV reporter Liz
5 Prefix for space
6 Brit's exclamation
7 Ultimate degree
8 President __
9 Architect Saarinen
10 Gad about
11 __ Lanka
12 Lazybones
13 Alabama city
14 Lock of hair
18 "__ intended"
22 "__ Ben Jonson"
23 Critic Kenneth
24 Not "fer"
25 Mideast airline
26 Chest protectors
27 Silents star
28 Error's partner
29 Like Alaska?
30 Ambler and Idle
34 *Captain* __ (Flynn film)
35 Fasting times
36 Coup d'__
38 "__ lay me down . . ."
39 Energetic
41 Like some cereals
44 Partiality
45 Opera immortal
46 Puts together
47 Word of regret
48 Easily bent
52 Sandwich shop
53 Barbell material
54 "If __ make it there . . ."
55 Gather, in chemistry
57 Use an axe
58 Big bird
59 Not refined
60 Spot for a cartographe
61 Good-for-nothing

83 BODY LANGUAGE

by Bob Lubbers

ACROSS

1 Acting job
5 Greek column style
10 Aid in crime
14 On top of
15 Stew style
16 Cabbie's take
17 Sports stadium
19 USC rival
20 Capture a fish
21 Mean one
23 Church area
26 *Billboard* entry
27 Alda and King
30 Bible line: Abbr.
32 *Father Knows Best* actress
35 Stable parent
36 Western capital
38 __ Zedong
39 Nimitz's rank: Abbr.
40 Chafes
41 Sprint rival
42 Iced drink
43 La Cosa __
44 Planting ground
45 Gold bar
47 Shoe width
48 Batters' ploys
49 Oklahoma city
51 Faint
53 Back-of-book sections
56 Brook's big brother
60 Pedestal part
61 Small rodent
64 Venerable prep school
65 Divided nation
66 Thailand, once
67 *My Three __* (sitcom)
68 Take the wheel
69 Relaxed state

DOWN

1 German valley
2 Ronny Howard role
3 Run easily
4 Board a Boeing
5 "They __ Believe Me"
6 Bobby of hockey
7 __ de Janeiro
8 Doctrines
9 Atkins and Huntley
10 __ *Thing Happened on the Way . . .*
11 Board game
12 Writer Gardner
13 Run like crazy
18 Stops from squeaking
22 Midwest Indians
24 Reluctant (to)
25 Tells a story
27 Violin maker
28 Burdened
29 Ultimate battle
31 Made a new sketch
33 Not spoken
34 Works hard
36 Cable channel
37 Teachers' grp.
40 Playful trick
44 __ *at Campobello*
46 Burger topping
48 The two of them
50 Ship strata
52 Mr. de la Renta
53 Midmonth day
54 Alliance acronym
55 Took a photo of
57 Director Kazan
58 Regretful word
59 Fictional aunt
62 Anger
63 Society-page word

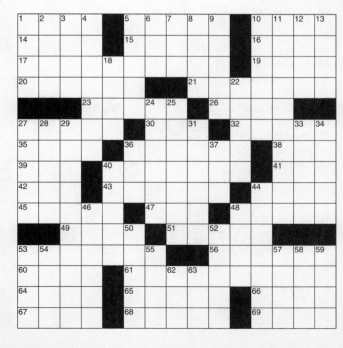

by Wayne R. Williams

ACROSS

1 Part of speech
5 Map collection
10 Smack hard
14 *Beetle Bailey* dog
15 Requirements
16 Lamb's pen name
17 Yuppie TV series
20 Common Market abbr.
21 Deep voices
22 Lets up
23 Northern constellation
25 Statuesque
27 Poker stakes
31 In advance
35 Milne book
39 Steno book
40 Egyptian bird
41 First course
42 British Isles republic
43 Gold container
44 Janis Ian tune of '75
46 Turkish export
48 Car choice
49 *Scarlett* setting
51 Noted virologist
55 English racecourse
58 Much loved
62 Yoko __
63 Beatles tune of '67
66 Solitary
67 Eagle's nest
68 Old Testament book
69 Drunkards
70 Editorial commands
71 Sleep symbols

DOWN

1 Widely recognized
2 Additional
3 New York city
4 Scand. land
5 Writer Seton
6 Hardy heroine
7 Most August-born folks
8 Own up to
9 Compass dir.
10 Sake
11 Wallach and Whitney
12 "Come here often?" is one
13 Merchandise labels
18 Steak cut
19 Fax ancestor
24 Crow cries
26 Tolerated
28 Winery worker
29 Time periods
30 Graf rival
32 Mayberry kid
33 Few and far between
34 First place
35 Puppy bites
36 Bassoon kin
37 Clever people
38 Computer command
42 Sicilian volcano
44 Cremona craftsman
45 Villainous
47 Makes amends
50 Selling feature
52 Rotgut
53 Become accustomed
54 Dunn and Ephron
55 Hole-making tools
56 "Skedaddle!"
57 Minimum change
59 Cable element
60 Cinema sign
61 Summers on the Somme
64 Bell and Barker
65 Shriner's topper

85 ON HAND

by Randolph Ross

ACROSS

1 Jocular sounds
5 Stopwatch, for instance
10 Counterfeit
13 ___ *Three Lives*
14 Pull out
15 Lea lady
16 California city
18 Anchorman Rather
19 Nearly alike
20 Auto center
22 Dwelt
24 Small salamanders
25 Chipped in
28 Physique, for short
29 Rag-doll name
30 "Boola" relative
31 Jarreau and Jolson
32 Like short plays
35 Punch in the mouth
39 African native
40 UN agcy.
41 Bit of deceit
42 ___ around (wander)
43 *Playboy* founder's nickname
44 Washbowl
46 Asian sea
48 Pinta was one
50 Tries to persuade
52 Young or Swit
56 "What a good boy ___!"
57 Sponge cakes
59 Wine variety
60 "On ___ Day"
61 Curriculum part
62 Rudolph's mother
63 Sharpens
64 Comics possum

DOWN

1 Pants supports
2 Jai ___
3 Pilot's place
4 Look up to
5 Like Ivan
6 ___ on parle français
7 Repaired
8 Moved sideways
9 Take it easy
10 Fakir's mattress
11 Anticipate
12 Fender benders
14 Fitness centers
17 Snow glider
21 Extend a subscription
23 Secret file
25 Places of refuge
26 Prefix for second
27 Hitchhike
29 In addition
31 Mr. Baba
32 Yoko ___
33 One-fifth of MX
34 At that time
36 Seal a tub
37 Dutch airline
38 Forage plants
43 Teacup part
44 European capital
45 Give ___ (assist)
46 Honor
47 Shakespearean teen
48 Football job
49 ___ dire (jury-selection process)
51 Cabbage product
53 ___' clock (midmorning)
54 Math subject
55 Legalese phrase
58 So far

86 THE DOCTOR IS IN

by Eric Albert

ACROSS

1 Small songbird
5 Societal no-no
10 Quite luxurious
14 Give a job to
15 Squirrel snack
16 Singer Guthrie
17 Dr. Seuss book
20 Wind instrument
21 Make mad
22 Newsman Koppel
23 Hoosegow
24 Trite writings
28 Like some hair
29 Mouth piece
32 Series of steps
33 *Of __ I Sing*
34 Mediocre
35 Dr. Seuss book
38 Actress Bancroft
39 Tehran's country
40 Leered at
41 NBA coach Unseld
42 Half hitch or bowline
43 Expressionless
44 Meditate (on)
45 Sock part
46 Formal wear
49 Latin prayer
54 Dr. Seuss book
56 Words of understanding
57 Fencing swords
58 Moore of *Ghost*
59 People
60 Mean and malicious
61 Kemo __

DOWN

1 Propeller's sound
2 Teeming (with)
3 Author Ambler
4 Roman emperor
5 Two-person bike
6 Played a part
7 Physicist Niels
8 Lode load
9 Cursory cleaning
10 Ward off
11 '77 whale movie
12 Hit hard
13 Stockings
18 Conductor Toscanini
19 Deep black
23 Song of praise
24 "Fiddlesticks!"
25 Make up (for)
26 Where livestock live
27 Beer adjective
28 Golden grain
29 Bloodhound features
30 Embers, eventually
31 *Bananas* name
33 Lose on purpose
34 It's a long story
36 XIX
37 Serious and somber
42 Aga __
43 Take it slow
44 Kiss target
45 Station receiver
46 End-of-week remark
47 Roughly
48 Orange cover
49 Ripens, as cheese
50 Tags on
51 Perlman of *Cheers*
52 Poetic foot
53 French friend
55 Valedictorian's pride: Abbr.

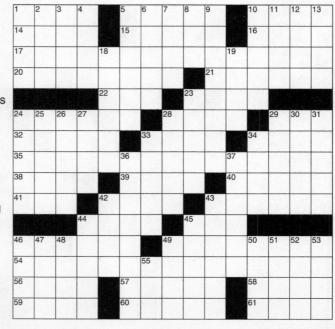

87 PLACES TO PLAY

by Wayne R. Williams

ACROSS

1 Jazzman Waller
5 Nonfilling dessert
10 Confused states
14 Vicinity
15 More frosty
16 Honolulu shindig
17 Fruit coat
18 Palmer's place
20 Country's count
22 Recording medium
23 Inventor Howe
24 Second ltr. addition
26 Open, in a way
30 Al Capp beast
32 Fur wrap
33 Gretzky's place
37 Clever person
38 Yoko __
39 Go bad
40 Miami Bch. road
42 Pasture
43 Hosp. area
44 Holyfield's place
47 More certain
50 Evasive maneuver
51 Tropical fish
52 Author LeShan
53 Barely beat
56 Filled with breezes
58 Small tree
59 Winter Olympics place

64 Past due
65 Cleveland's lake
66 Explosive, for short
67 Genesis name
68 Fetches
69 Prepare to drive
70 Family rooms

DOWN

1 Broad comedy
2 Statesman Sharon
3 Seles' place
4 Inept soldier
5 Lively dances
6 Coll. major
7 Diamond lady
8 Some jabs
9 Dangerous whale
10 Well-versed
11 __ *Miss Brooks*
12 Flivver fuel
13 Take to court
19 Musical work
21 Stadium seater
24 __ Alegre, Brazil
25 Taro product
27 Striker's place
28 Little green man
29 Price twice
31 Advice-column initials
33 Lifting device
34 When actors enter

35 Mrs. Yeltsin
36 Good-natured
41 Think alike
45 Marked a ballot
46 Became flushed
48 Wipes off
49 Metal rod
52 Singer Gorme
54 Iacocca's successor
55 Clothe oneself
57 Monthly check
58 Queue before Q
59 Canine command
60 Unrefined metal
61 Wee amount
62 Hwy.
63 S.A. nation

88 TWENTY QUESTIONS

by S.N.

ACROSS

1 Spill the beans
5 MacLeod of *The Love Boat*
10 Word on a fuse
14 Actress Anderson
15 Singer Cara
16 Kingly address
17 Rolaids target
18 Light beer
19 Get __ the ground floor
20 What the Mets play at Shea
22 Least usual
24 Fuss
25 Phone co.
27 Comparative suffix
28 Twelfth letter
30 Has at
33 Writer Burrows
36 Filmed a new version of
38 Ankle adornment
40 Ending for opt
41 Charles' princedom
43 First name
44 Scout's asset
46 "Be __ your school"
48 Thesaurus find: Abbr.
49 Punctilious
51 Omega's preceder
52 Mr. Wallach
54 Slinger's handful
55 Word form for "equal"
57 Sense
60 Court players
64 It's east of the Urals
65 Governor Stevenson
67 Robert De __
68 Catch some rays
69 Runner Steve
70 __ end (over)
71 Grade-school homework
72 Where things are
73 Cosby's first series

DOWN

1 Not very interesting
2 Plumb crazy
3 Charisma
4 Waited awhile
5 Arizona river
6 One of the Musketeers
7 Meatless main course
8 -esque relative
9 Pianist Peter
10 Out of the way
11 Ore veins
12 Big leaguers
13 Transmitted
21 Egg on
23 Half of DJ
26 Akron product
28 Onetime Indians
29 General Curtis __
31 Underground passage
32 Holds up
34 Overcomes
35 "Me too," in Montreal
37 100%
39 __ de cologne
42 Morning, à la Winchell
45 Grand-scale
47 Jockey's controller
50 Have thoughts
53 Pipe problems
56 Mideast region
57 Little bits
58 Jacob's twin
59 New Mexico town
61 What criticizers pick
62 Corner
63 Panasonic rival
66 A third of MDXVIII

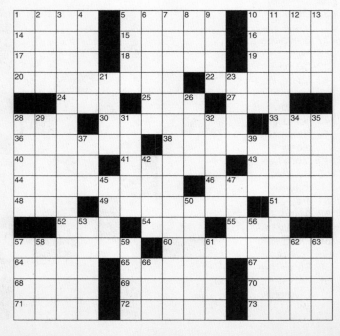

by Trip Payne

ACROSS

1 Behold, to Brutus
5 James and Kett
10 Prejudice
14 "__ I say, not . . ."
15 Precious kids
16 Mrs. Lindbergh
17 Book protector
19 Thurmond of basketball
20 Country music?
21 Makes captive
23 Act as pilot
24 Chicago's zone: Abbr.
25 Santa __, CA
26 Bring up
28 Geronimo, for one
31 Cornfield cries
34 Some cars
37 Former Mideast nation: Abbr.
38 High __ kite
39 Ratfink
40 Coffee brewer
41 __ Misérables
42 Quitter's word
43 Iowa city
44 Composer Gustav
46 Jamie of M*A*S*H
48 Franklin's nickname
49 Dietary component
51 Actress Slezak
55 Outer limit
58 Dotes on
59 Pasturelands
60 Important time for networks
62 Memo phrase
63 Gives for a time
64 Feminine ending
65 Pea holders
66 Use the delete key
67 Owner's proof

DOWN

1 Icelandic classics
2 Make a difference
3 Social position
4 Williams and Rolle
5 Gouda alternative
6 Gumshoe
7 Can hold
8 Don't exist
9 Concordes, e.g.
10 Split need
11 Where sound can't travel
12 Chip in
13 Understands
18 Burns of *Dear John*
22 Slip-up
24 *Antigone* king
27 "Swinging on __"
28 Ms. Bryant
29 Krishna preceder
30 Ocean fliers
31 Not upset
32 Taking a cruise
33 Kind of stomach
35 Put on
36 High above
39 Bloodhound's track
43 Like a one-way sign
45 Camera parts
47 Cincinnati team
49 Not so many
50 Sports palace
52 Actress Dunne
53 New Hampshire city
54 Was inquisitive
55 Gymnast's maneuver
56 Betting setting
57 Capri is one
58 Church area
61 Bradley and Begley

90 WALL COVERING NEEDS

by Bob Lubbers

ACROSS

1. *Casablanca* role
5. Pay out
10. Practice punching
14. Arthur of tennis
15. Rarin' to go
16. Top of the head
17. Loco
19. Enjoying the Love Boat
20. Like some steel
21. Bent a fender
23. __ October (fictional sub)
24. Painter/inventor
25. Sitter hirer
29. Board-game pair
30. Troop grp.
33. Likeness
34. Rope twist
35. Hockey target
36. Judy's daughter
37. Mails away
38. Rajah's spouse
39. School founded in 1440
40. Poker card
41. __ blanche
42. Leb. neighbor
43. Phobos orbits it
44. Make angry
45. Not much, so to speak
47. Josh around
48. Was generous
50. Work together
55. Elite alternative
56. Harmless loudmouth
58. Varieties
59. Way to the altar
60. Scarlett's home
61. Airplane tip
62. Equine gaits
63. Pretentious

DOWN

1. All ears
2. Cartographer's speck
3. Good buddy
4. Bush Cabinet member
5. Covert
6. Peeled off
7. Old oath
8. Pince-__ glasses
9. Ship-repair spots
10. Reaches across
11. Paper product
12. Suited to __
13. Perused
18. Swiss city
22. Poetic preposition
24. Mork's friend
25. Lots (of)
26. Friendliness
27. Arkansas athletes
28. Actor Richard
29. Eats in style
31. "A votre __!"
32. Green-card holder
34. Deborah and Graham
35. Alumnus
37. Take no more cards
41. West Pointer
43. Miss West
44. British bishops' hats
46. Rub out
47. Prepared to be knighted
48. Joyride
49. Hawaiian city
50. __ facto
51. Comedian Rudner
52. Seaweed product
53. Part of CD
54. Serving piece
57. Make public

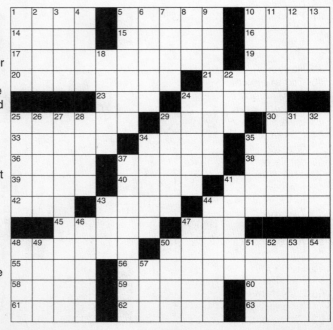

PULLING RANK

by Eric Albert

ACROSS

1 Social blunder
6 "This can't be!"
10 Mistake-maker's cry
14 Expect
15 Way out
16 Give a hand
17 Doctor's career
20 Brontë heroine
21 List entry
22 Extend a subscription
23 Tuna holders
25 Touch against
27 State strongly
30 Trojan War hero
31 Violinist's need
34 Classic Western film
35 Computer owner
36 Clown character
37 Bob Keeshan role
40 European range
41 Weave a web
42 In unison
43 Single layer
44 Day laborer
45 Gas-range part
46 Cry
47 Eight furlongs
48 In the know
51 In the know about
53 Not at all stiff
57 Long-running soap opera
60 Hardwood trees
61 Couple
62 Knot again
63 Irritating insect
64 First name in mysteries
65 Days __ (yore)

DOWN

1 Stare openmouthed
2 Out of whack
3 County event
4 Words on a nickel
5 Greek letter
6 *Waiting for Lefty* playwright
7 Clinton's hometown
8 Marilyn's real name
9 "...man __ mouse?"
10 Eightsome
11 Lena of *Havana*
12 Leaders set it
13 Gush forth
18 Delicate color
19 Key point
24 General vicinity
26 Horse's home
27 Composers' org.
28 "__ We Dance?"
29 Foolish
30 Invite to stay
31 Element #5
32 Layer in the news
33 Swain
35 Not much liked
36 Sculpture variety
38 Understanding words
39 Caesar's conquest
44 Jury member
45 Storage boxes
46 Take by force
47 007 portrayer
48 Excited
49 Withdraw (from)
50 "Lonely Boy" singer
52 Mr. Donahue
54 "Tell __ the judge!"
55 Body armor
56 Said "guilty," perhaps
58 Tailless simian
59 In favor of

92 FLAG-WAVING

by David A. Davidson

ACROSS

1 Lip service of a sort
5 'Tis, in the past
9 Wearied
14 Add to the pot
15 Indian chief
16 Green shade
17 Ballet bend
18 Russian river
19 O-shaped roll
20 Flag-hoisting contests?
23 Storm
24 Adorn an i
25 Cry of contempt
28 Kon-Tiki Museum locale
31 Cash alternative
33 Arctic or Antarctic
37 Director Preminger
39 Boxer Max
40 "Flag Factory Robbed"?
43 Pain in the neck
44 Change course
45 Gets an apartment
46 St. Francis' home
48 Ready to pick
50 Author Buscaglia
51 Summer in Quebec
53 Pacific island
58 Flag day?
61 Set firmly
64 Adverse fate
65 Eban of Israel
66 Having knowledge
67 Science mag
68 Bridge support
69 Less outdated
70 Shoe inserts
71 Injury

DOWN

1 Key letter
2 Shore recess
3 Be frugal
4 "You look as if you've ___ ghost!"
5 Swimwear
6 Toad feature
7 Open a bit
8 Bar food
9 Williams of *Poltergeist*
10 Word of regret
11 Use a backhoe
12 Garden dweller
13 Pa. neighbor
21 Squash variety
22 Tropical bean
25 Einstein
26 Artist's rep
27 Toast beginning
29 Traditional knowledge
30 Supplementary
32 Well-qualified
33 From John Paul
34 Corpulent
35 Cow catcher
36 One of the opposition
38 Actress Garr
41 Señora Perón
42 Be apprehensive about
47 Bird dog
49 Authorize
52 The ___ the line
54 Bacterium type
55 Leg bone
56 Barbecue leftover
57 Get guns again
58 Kingly address
59 Circular roof
60 First-rate
61 Omelet cooker
62 Be a mortgagor
63 Got a peek at

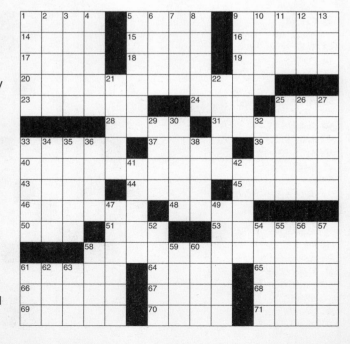

93 ZOO FILMS

by Eric Albert

ACROSS

1 __ Having a Baby
5 Suitor
10 Iced dessert
14 Roof edge
15 "Stormy Weather" singer
16 Ballerina Pavlova
17 Hepburn film of '68
20 Music character
21 Unbind
22 "__ the season . . ."
23 Emmy-winner Daly
24 Mature woman
28 Cuts the grass
29 *Murphy Brown* network
32 Circle the earth
33 Toll road
34 Dr. Jonas __
35 Hogan film of '86
38 Bumper-sticker word
39 Religious image
40 *M*A*S*H* extra
41 Inspire wonder
42 Sounds of censure
43 Optimally
44 Slow and dull
45 Act human?
46 Professional penman
49 Help hatch
54 Heston film of '68
56 Become a landlord
57 Locker-room garment
58 Milan money
59 __ Ono
60 Nail-board stuff
61 Entrée list

DOWN

1 Abel's brother
2 Laughing sounds
3 Mr. Knievel
4 Prefix for propelled
5 Sure winner
6 Usual practices
7 Auto-racer Luyendyk
8 Tavern or hotel
9 Yesterday's groom
10 Lake craft
11 Picnic pests
12 Anatomical hinge
13 Deserve for deeds
18 Wholly
19 Charged particles
23 Small souvenir
24 Fudge flavor
25 Quiver contents
26 Steak cut
27 *Casablanca* character
28 Director Forman
29 Core group
30 Glorify
31 Trapshooter's target
33 Overly exacting
34 Social slight
36 Data holder
37 Not so
42 Fit-tied link
43 In a mischievous manner
44 Kind of bean
45 Go into
46 Vigorously active
47 Singer Laine
48 Foul-smelling
49 "__ Only Have Love"
50 Soothing cream
51 ". . . baked in __"
52 Sea swallow
53 Birthright seller
55 Pah-pah preceder

94 STAGE NAMES

by Fred Piscop

ACROSS

1 Señor's squiggle
6 __ *Richard's Almanack*
10 Sp. woman
13 Indian, for one
14 __ snuff (acceptable)
15 Recipe component
16 BERNARD SCHWARTZ
18 Order for dinner
19 Cool treat
20 More harsh
22 Taurus preceder
24 As Darth Vader would
25 Gunboat feature
28 Discoverer's cry
30 Patella locale
31 At any time
33 Extends one's enlistment
36 Peculiar
37 "Inner" word form
38 US draftees
40 Cheerleading word
41 __ as a judge
43 Small songbird
45 Prefix for nautical
46 Turmoil
48 Man with a megaphone
50 George C. Scott role
52 Mideast rulers
54 Decks out
56 South American airline
60 Gator kin
61 RICHARD STARKEY
63 Fork prong
64 Secluded valley
65 Lama land
66 __ in "solve"
67 Exercise system
68 Caravan stops

DOWN

1 Little shavers
2 Sect's symbol
3 Arsenio Hall rival
4 Preschoolers' supervision
5 Bonus piece
6 Thick soup
7 Pick
8 Elevator man
9 Player list
10 ARTHUR JEFFERSON
11 Party hearty
12 Mimic's skill
15 Gray bird
17 Puts together
21 New York's Medgar __ College
23 Visualize
25 Ring results
26 Take apart
27 AARON CHWATT
29 Egg on
32 Solemn promises
34 Trim off
35 Brake device
37 Shortstop's slip
39 Not outside the body
42 Tempt
44 Numbered hwy.
45 Old French region
47 Get-up-and-go
49 Brit noble
50 Nation's agreements
51 High-ceiling courts
53 __ Carta
55 Missile housing
57 Captures
58 Native Canadian
59 They may be liberal
62 Electron's chg.

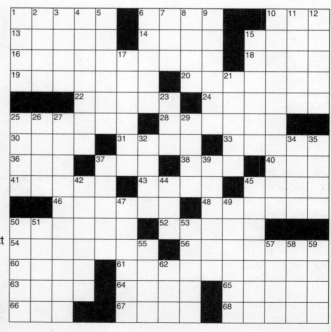

95 ALL WET

by Eric Albert

ACROSS

1 Historical period
4 Cup of coffee
8 Betrayed boredom
14 Actor Herbert
15 *Exodus* author
16 The List of __ Messenger
17 Rock Hudson film of '68
20 Oedipus' mother
21 Maui strings
22 Needing a massage
23 __ en scène (stage setting)
25 Diplomacy
29 Farm tool
30 Tornado, so to speak
33 Pigeon sound
34 18th President
35 Wife's mom, e.g.
37 Chinese-food ingredient
41 Family car
42 Indian corn
43 Night before
44 *La Mer* composer
47 "Tea for __"
50 Horn sound
52 Sleeveless garment
53 Impatient one's query
54 Clark's coworker
56 Color close to cranberry
59 Old-time engine
63 French mathematician
64 Owl outburst
65 Singer Damone
66 Main road
67 Poet Millay
68 Doe beau

DOWN

1 Biblical prophet
2 Art genre
3 *Cocoon* Oscar-winner
4 Sticks out
5 Smell __ (be suspicious)
6 Pauling's specialty
7 "__ was saying . . ."
8 American Leaguer
9 Ax cousin
10 Twist violently
11 Pen point
12 Corn unit
13 Heredity letters
18 Pronounce
19 Kick out
24 Panama, for one
26 Rights org.
27 Paint layer
28 Aspen machine
30 Tendency
31 Kid's card game
32 Real swank
34 Onetime sports car
36 Compass pt.
37 Sand-castle destroyer
38 Film critic James
39 Dirty Harry portrayer
40 Sibling, for short
41 Spider product
45 As Satan would
46 Kiss: Sp.
47 Be prosperous
48 Cotton killer
49 At bat next
51 Finish second
53 Drenched
55 Actor Sharif
57 "__ Fire" (Springsteen song)
58 __ bene
59 Health center
60 Paving material
61 Superlative suffix
62 Señor Guevara

ALL THINGS BRIGHT

by Richard Silvestri

ACROSS

1 Midway attraction
5 Sound of fright
9 Robin Cook book
13 In a while
14 No-no
15 More than
16 Bowling, New England-style
18 Zola novel
19 Charm
20 Chow down
21 Black card
22 Echo
24 Standard charge
26 Heads the cast
28 Parking place
32 Tesh colleague
35 Facial feature
37 "Born in the __"
38 Procedure
39 Pub potation
40 Attacking with satire
45 Cleveland or Washington: Abbr.
46 Come into view
47 Hefty
49 Real bummer
51 As __ pin
55 '60s TV talker
58 __-Magnon man
60 Gets around
61 Univ. unit
62 Barge crew
64 Up to it
65 New York island
66 Where to see FDR
67 __-do-well
68 Gravity-powered vehicle
69 Ending for joke or game

DOWN

1 Indy entrant
2 Senseless
3 Ladies of Spain
4 Last
5 Big difference
6 Rose lover of fiction
7 Sub device
8 Mail-order extra
9 Anxiety
10 Sort of circular
11 Café handout
12 Riyadh resident
14 Threefold
17 Boorish fellow
23 Tied
25 Roof goo
27 Slowpoke
29 Not quite shut
30 Strong wind
31 Flock females
32 Luau lesson
33 PDQ kin
34 Gangplank
36 Critic Kenneth
41 Pushcart proprietor
42 Regatta need
43 Wise guys
44 Welcomes
45 Kinds of firecrackers
48 Was resilient
50 Cross-examine
52 Own up to
53 "Come up and __"
54 Actor Ed
55 Thom of shoedom
56 After-bath wear
57 Fashion mag
59 Make eyes at
63 Took cover

by Shirley Soloway

ACROSS

1 Five-time Wimbledon champ
5 Hurt badly
9 Small pieces
13 Lhasa's locale
14 Ms. Abzug
15 "Put a lid __!"
16 Doesn't exist
17 TV studio sign
18 Theda of silents
19 Quite appropriate
22 Dr. Casey
23 Leave behind
24 Singer Barbara
26 Beef cut
28 __ Field (old Brooklyn ballpark)
31 Breakfast order
34 Vicinity
37 Tatum or Ryan
38 "That's awesome!"
39 Act of deception
41 San Diego attraction
42 Conductor Dorati
44 Withdraw (from)
45 Constant irritant
46 Wetter, in a way
48 Hire a decorator
50 Thrust upon
53 Draws out
57 Play on words
59 Make a great impression
61 *M*A*S*H* star
63 Yes ending
64 Sea flier
65 Privy to
66 Took a crack at
67 Vex
68 Flat craft
69 Dance move
70 Editor's instruction

DOWN

1 Puppeteer Bil
2 Actor Davis
3 Christmas-song quintet
4 Gets together
5 Haberdashery department
6 Warning sound
7 Sacro follower
8 Leatherneck
9 Short haircut
10 Very easily
11 Grow weary
12 Ollie's buddy
14 Rudder operator
20 Capote's nickname
21 Big shot
25 King __ Saud
27 Ship's forepart
29 New Mexico town
30 Pigeonhole
31 Old oath
32 Heredity unit
33 Hear about
35 Ram's mate
36 Slightly open
39 Sacked out
40 Kind of jack
43 Purpose
45 Sulky ones
47 Cooks chestnuts
49 Tooth pro's deg.
51 Mini, for one
52 Very strange
54 French painter
55 Comic Kovacs
56 Refine metal
57 Matched set
58 Forearm bone
60 Horn sound
62 Ubiquitous bug

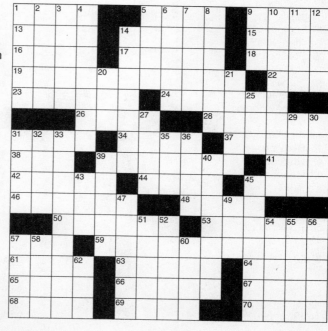

POLITICS AS USUAL

by Richard Silvestri

ACROSS

1 Pompous people
6 Where the Vikings landed
10 Riga resident
14 Written exercise
15 Smart guy?
16 Hodgepodge
17 Gobbled up
18 *Educating* ___ ('83 film)
19 Secluded valley
20 Political PR person
22 Hard to find
23 It may be legal
24 Slots spot
26 Change chemically
29 Make happy
33 Spheres
37 Hodges of baseball
38 Something to sneeze at?
39 Collect the crops
40 Alpha's antithesis
42 Major Hoople's cry
43 Prohibit by law
45 Bern's river
46 NFL team
47 Connecting flight
48 Opposition group
50 Principal role
52 MCI rival
57 Not as much
60 Political operative
63 Grad
64 Author James
65 More than

66 Crib cry
67 "Them" or "Us"
68 Mystic writings
69 In a while
70 One of the gang
71 Oscar-night sight

DOWN

1 Bikini event
2 Physical condition
3 Become established
4 Correct a text
5 "Return to ___"
6 Painter Chagall
7 Came to earth
8 Snappy comeback
9 Make quake
10 Political crony
11 Ms. Fitzgerald
12 Section of seats
13 Color variation
21 The Beaver State
25 Modernizing prefix
27 Fire preceder
28 Unsullied
30 Pond life
31 Stagecoach puller
32 Tackle's colleagues
33 Metallic rocks
34 Find a tenant
35 ___ California
36 Political opportunist
38 Louisiana county

41 Gunsel's weapon
44 Fury
48 Musically slow
49 Asparagus units
51 Flooded
53 Answer a charge
54 Actress Massey
55 "When pigs fly!"
56 Lock of hair
57 Prayer-wheel user
58 Zing
59 Big-time wrestling?
61 Take it from the top
62 Homeowner's holding

by Fred Piscop

ACROSS
1 Puccini opera
6 Biblical king
11 __ Paulo, Brazil
14 Detest
15 Full of energy
16 "__ a boy!"
17 "That's All, Folks!" series
19 Meadow
20 Ponce de __
21 Conger
22 Mark again
24 Mr. Sharif
26 "__ Back to Old Virginny"
27 Max of makeup
30 Convertible, slangily
31 *The Lady* __
32 Rayburn and Kelly
33 Unexplained sighting
36 Greek H's
37 Hand-cream additives
38 Short distance
39 Shriner's topper
40 Ships' staffs
41 Absolute
42 Naval aide
44 Drearily
45 Bone-dry
47 "Purple __" (Prince tune)
48 Total (to)
49 Dinghy need
50 Info
54 __ es Salaam
55 Sunday-news insert
58 Foolish fellow
59 Poetic muse

60 Shriver of TV
61 Mao __-tung
62 __ *Seed* ('77 movie)
63 Jazz dance

DOWN
1 Hard to believe
2 Orchestra member
3 "Get lost!"
4 Implies
5 "__ you serious?"
6 Bigot, for one
7 Hebrew month
8 __ Tin Tin
9 Excess supplies
10 Just __ (punishment)
11 Pliable toy
12 *The* __ (Mr. T series)
13 American Indian
18 Planetary lap
23 To opposite
25 Stylish, so to speak
26 Bamboolike grasses
27 Feudal estate
28 Feed the kitty
29 Custer opponent
30 Take title to anew
32 Gather slowly
34 Sense
35 Grand Ole __
37 Generator part

38 Maintain one's position
40 Like some beef
41 Mentalist Geller
43 __ Claire, WI
44 Robin Williams role
45 Camp David Accords signer
46 Collect
47 Semi-synthetic fabric
49 Aware of
51 Dynamic start
52 Barbershop order
53 PDQ
56 Asian nation, for short
57 Mornings: Abbr.

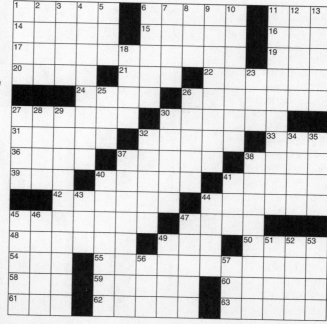

100 WATER PIX

by Alice Long

ACROSS

1 Go for a rathskeller record
5 __ as a hatter
10 Hacienda home
14 Looking up
15 __ la Paix (Paris street)
16 Polly or Mame
17 "Excuse me!"
18 More fitting
19 The Lettermen, e.g.
20 Book of pride and Joy?
22 Sham
24 Controversial tree spray
25 Feed the hogs
26 Action film of '80
33 Ham it up
34 Steno's boss
35 Hamper fill
36 "Uh-uh!"
37 Loft lava
38 Actress Zetterling
39 Airport stats.
41 Rocky peaks
42 Gather bit by bit
44 War film of '60
47 Woolly moms
48 Bridge section
49 Drawing room
52 Hold one's hand?
56 End-of-scene direction
57 Gourmand
59 *Star Trek VI* captain
60 Chorus singer
61 States
62 Iowa State address
63 Low in fat
64 Breach of judgment
65 Staple to a board

DOWN

1 Hermit by the sea
2 Jocular sounds
3 Computer owner
4 Olympics entrant
5 Ark docking site
6 Comics crew
7 Distribute
8 Wine-cooler base
9 Ghost ship
10 Unwitting tool
11 Ambiance
12 Ornery mood
13 The gamut
21 Hightail it
23 Balderdash
25 Cinderella characters
26 Clair and Auberjonois
27 Stradivari's teacher
28 Grant Wood was one
29 Commuter's home
30 Finger-pointer
31 Esau's father
32 Armor flaw
37 Otherworldly
40 Hope contemporary
42 FBI employee
43 Map-making Earth orbiter
45 Early afternoon
46 Thinly distributed
49 Ring out
50 Linchpin locale
51 Beatles' meter maid
52 Plan part
53 Wild cat
54 Sir Guinness
55 Walrus feature
58 Rock-video award

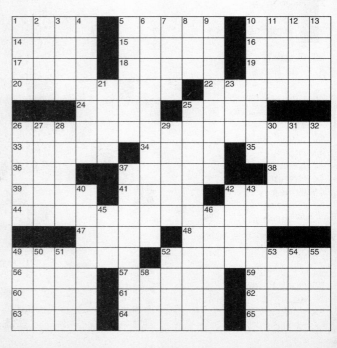

PORTABLE, AFFORDABLE CROSSWORDS *from* RANDOM HOUSE

Each selection features 100 fun and easy crosswords presented in a convenient package. These puzzles are sure to delight anyone who's on the go or just on a break. Wherever you plan to be, make sure you have one of these portable volumes by your side.

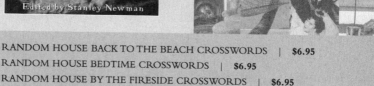

ANSWERS

1

A	L	P	S		S	C	R	A	M		C	A	S	T
C	A	L	M		Q	U	O	T	A		O	N	O	R
I	N	A	U	G	U	R	A	T	I	O	N	D	A	Y
D	E	N		R	E	E	D		N	A	D	I	R	
			G	O	A	D		A	L	T	O			
A	T	R	I	S	K		B	L	A	H		A	N	T
T	A	I	L	S		A	R	O	N		W	O	O	
O	F	F	T	O	A	G	O	O	D	S	T	A	R	T
N	F	L		M	E	A	N		A	R	I	S	E	
E	Y	E		L	A	N	D		P	R	O	T	E	M
			P	O	R	T		S	L	O	T			
	M	A	R	I	E		D	O	I	N		D	U	D
B	E	G	I	N	T	H	E	B	E	G	U	I	N	E
B	R	E	D		T	A	M	E	R		M	A	T	E
C	E	D	E		O	D	O	R	S		P	L	O	P

2

C	L	A	W		O	T	I	S		E	D	N	A	S
L	I	M	A		P	E	T	E		G	R	A	T	E
E	L	A	N		E	L	S	E		G	U	I	L	E
F	I	N	G	E	R	L	A	K	E	S		L	A	M
			L	E	E	S		S	H	R	E	W	S	
I	N	T	E	N	T		R	E	S	E	N	D		
F	A	H	D		T	O	U	T		L	A	D		
S	T	U		P	A	L	M	O	I	L		O	L	E
	M	E	L		D	O	N	S		T	W	I	N	
B	R	A	Y	E	R		G	R	A	N	D	S		
F	L	E	E	C	E		S	O	A	R				
R	E	L		K	N	U	C	K	L	E	H	E	A	D
O	V	I	N	E		C	L	A	D		E	L	S	A
S	E	N	A	T		L	A	T	E		E	M	I	T
T	R	A	P	S		A	M	E	N		L	O	S	E

3

L	A	G	S		J	U	A	N		D	A	M	E	
A	B	O	U		M	A	G	M	A		E	V	E	N
B	Y	E	B	Y	E	B	L	A	C	K	B	I	R	D
S	E	N	S	E	N		I	N	H	O	U	S	E	
			E	N	O	S		S	O	O	T			
P	A	R	T		T	H	E		S	L	I	T	S	
A	D	A		S	T	A	R	E		A	N	A	M	E
C	H	I	C	H	I	R	O	D	R	I	G	U	E	Z
T	O	S	E	A		E	D	G	E	D		P	A	R
	C	A	N	N	Y		E	A	T		H	E	R	A
			T	A	O	S		R	I	T	E			
	B	R	I	N	G	O	N		R	I	A	L	T	O
M	A	U	M	A	U	R	E	B	E	L	L	I	O	N
E	L	S	E		R	E	M	U	S		T	R	O	T
T	I	E	S		T	R	O	D		H	A	L	O	

4

A	H	A	B		I	B	I	S		S	P	I	K	E
M	A	M	A		T	U	N	A		T	A	T	E	R
P	H	I	N	E	A	S	T	B	L	U	S	T	E	R
S	A	N	D	A	L		O	U	I		T	O	P	
			S	T	Y		B	R	A					
C	A	S	T	S		H	I	R	E		C	A	M	
U	C	L	A		C	L	A	R	A	B	E	L	L	E
S	T	A	N		O	I	L	E	R		R	O	L	L
H	O	W	D	Y	D	O	O	D	Y		G	N	A	T
Y	R	S		S	I	N	S		P	O	E	T	S	
			T	L	C		S	U	N					
M	A	O		I	S	A		A	B	O	D	E	S	
B	U	F	F	A	L	O	B	O	B	S	M	I	T	H
A	S	T	I	N		D	U	N	E		I	S	T	O
T	E	S	T	Y		A	M	E	R		C	H	E	W

5

B	M	I		S	A	D	A		D	O	M	O		
H	E	A	R		E	L	A	N		E	R	O	D	E
M	A	R	K	S	D	O	W	N		N	I	N	O	S
O	R	K		P	A	N	G		S	M	E	A	R	S
			I	C	I	N	G		C	H	A	N		
C	L	E	A	T	S		S	H	O	R	T	A	G	E
L	O	P	E	S		C	H	I	N	K		C	A	N
A	T	O	N		T	O	R	T	E		S	C	U	D
I	T	S		R	O	V	E	S		S	I	E	G	E
M	O	T	H	E	R	E	D		F	A	N	N	E	D
			O	M	A	R		C	R	U	E	T		
F	A	R	R	A	H		G	R	I	T		M	E	T
A	N	E	A	R		T	R	A	D	E	M	A	R	K
S	T	A	C	K		R	A	N	G		B	R	I	O
	I	D	E	S		I	S	E	E		A	K	C	

6

A	B	U	T	S		M	A	S	T		T	R	E	K
C	A	R	O	L		A	S	I	A		O	O	Z	E
T	R	A	F	A	L	G	A	R	S	Q	U	A	R	E
E	N	L	I	V	E	N		E	T	E	R	N	A	L
			V	E	T	O		N	E	D				
A	C	H	E		L	A	S		W	A	D	S		
B	R	A		O	T	I	S		S	P	I	N	E	T
B	E	R	M	U	D	A	T	R	I	A	N	G	L	E
O	T	T	E	R	S		R	E	N	T		E	L	I
T	E	E	N		T	A	D		F	R	A	N		
			B	O	A		F	A	T	E				
M	I	S	C	A	S	T		A	R	R	A	I	G	N
A	N	T	A	R	C	T	I	C	C	I	R	C	L	E
R	O	U	T		A	O	N	E		S	N	E	E	R
E	N	D	S		R	O	A	D		H	O	S	E	D

7

C	O	D	E		E	L	S	E		P	E	L	T	S
A	B	E	L		T	E	R	N		E	L	I	O	T
R	O	B	I	N	H	O	O	D		L	I	T	E	R
L	E	S	S	O	N		S	A	I	N	T			
			L	I	F	T		S	C	O	L	D		
M	A	N	A	C	L	E		P	A	R	E	R	S	
S	A	L	O	N		E	L	L	E	N		J	O	E
W	I	L	T		R	E	S	I	N		L	O	N	E
A	L	A		H	A	S	T	E		C	O	H	E	N
B	E	N	T	O	N		A	G	R	O	U	N	D
	D	A	R	L	A		R	E	E	L				
		D	E	L	T	A		C	O	S	T	A	S	
B	L	A	M	E		F	R	I	A	R	T	U	C	K
V	A	L	O	R		R	U	I	N		A	N	T	I
D	Y	E	R	S		O	M	I	T		R	E	S	T

8

W	E	A	K		S	T	E	V	E		S	H	A	G
A	R	O	N		T	O	T	A	L		N	I	N	E
W	I	N	I	N	A	W	A	L	K		E	T	T	A
A	C	E	T	A	T	E	S		H	A	R	P	E	R
				M	E	L		G	O	T	T	A		
H	A	S	T	E	N		B	A	U	M		Y	E	A
A	L	T	O	S		T	W	I	N		A	D	A	M
S	O	R	E		B	R	A	N	D		L	I	T	E
T	H	I	S		E	O	N	S		P	A	R	T	S
O	A	K		T	A	T	A		F	R	I	T	O	S
			E	V	E	R	S		D	R	U			
P	A	G	O	D	A		L	I	O	N	I	Z	E	S
A	L	O	T		B	R	E	E	Z	E	H	O	M	E
P	A	L	E		L	A	N	G	E		O	N	I	T
A	N	D	S		E	N	D	O	N		P	E	T	S

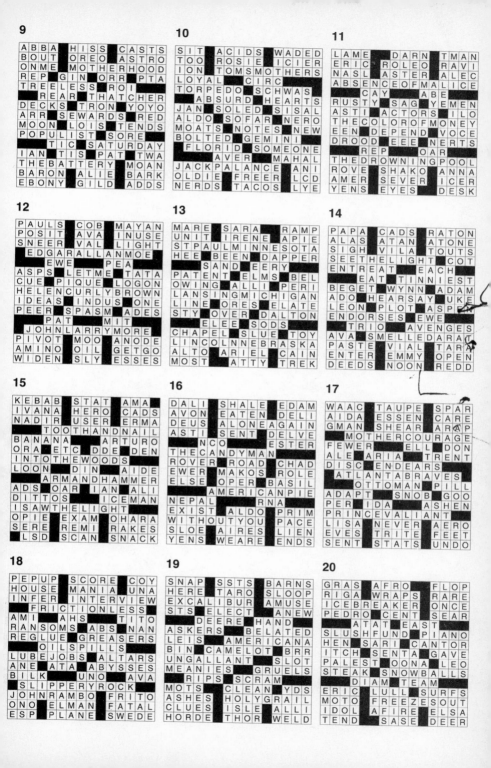

9

```
ABBA HISS CASTS
BOUT OREO ASTRO
ONME MOTHERHOOD
REP GIN ORR PTA
TREELESS ROI
REAR THATCHER
DECKS TRON YOYO
ARR SEWARDS RED
MOON LOIS TENDS
POPULIST SORE
TIC SATURDAY
IAN TIS PAT TWA
THEBATTERY MOAN
BARON ALIE BARK
EBONY GILD ADDS
```

10

```
SIT ACIDS WADED
TOO ROSIE ICIER
ION TOMSMOTHERS
LOYAL CIRC
TORPEDO SCHWAS
ABSURD HEARTS
JAN SOLED SISAL
ALDO SOFAR NERO
MOATS NOTES NEW
BOLTED GEMINI
FLORID SOMEONE
AVER MAHAL
JACKPALANCE ANI
OLDIE FREER LCD
NERDS TACOS LYE
```

11

```
LAME DARN TMAN
ERIC ROLEO RAVI
NASL ASTER ALEC
ABSENCEOFMALICE
CAY ABE
RUSTY SAG YEMEN
ASTI ACTORS ILO
THECOLOROFMONEY
EEN DEPEND VOCE
DROOD EEE NERTS
REP OAR
THEDROWNINGPOOL
ROVE SHAKO ANNA
AMER SEVER ICER
YENS EYES DESK
```

12

```
PAULS COB MAYAN
POSIT AVA INUSE
SNEER VAL LIGHT
EDGARALLANMOE
EWE PEA
ASPS LETME TATA
CUE PIQUE LOGON
HELENCURLYBROWN
IDEAS INDUS ONE
PEER SPASM ADES
PAT MIT
JOHNLARRYMORE
PIVOT MOO ANODE
AMINO OIL GETGO
WIDEN SLY ESSES
```

13

```
MARE SARA RAMP
UNIT IRENE APIE
STPAULMINNESOTA
HEE BEEN DAPPER
SAND EERY
PATENT ELMS BEL
OWING ALLI PERI
LANSINGMICHIGAN
LINE ORES ELATE
STY OVER DALTON
ELEE SODS
CHAPEL SLUE TOY
LINCOLNNEBRASKA
ALTO ARIEL CAIN
MOST ATTY TREK
```

14

```
PAPA CADS RATON
ALAS ATAN ATONE
SIGH VILA TOUTS
SEETHELIGHT COT
ENTREAT EACH
EAT TINNIEST
BEGET WYNN ADAM
ADO HEARSAY UKE
LEON PLOT ASPE
ENDORSES EWE
TRIO AVENGES
AVA SMELLEDARAT
PASTE VIAL TAR
ENTER EMMY OPEN
DEEDS NOON REDD
```

15

```
KEBAB STAT AMA
IVANA HERO CADS
NADIR USER ERMA
TOOTHANDNAIL
BANANA ARTURO
ORA ETC DDE DEN
INTOTHEWOODS
LOON DIN AIDE
ARMANDHAMMER
ADS OAR IAN ALI
DITTOS ICEMAN
ISAWTHELIGHT
OPIE EXAM OHARA
SERE REMI RAKES
LSD SCAN SNACK
```

16

```
DALI SHALE EDAM
AVON EATEN DELI
DEUS ALONEAGAIN
ASTI SENT DELVE
NCO ESTER
THECANDYMAN
ROVER ROAD CHAD
EWER MAKOS ROLE
ELSE OPER BASIL
AMERICANPIE
NEPAL RNA
EXIST ALDO PRIM
WITHOUTYOU PACE
SLOE AIRES LIEN
YENS WEARE ENDS
```

17

```
WAAC TAUPE SPAR
AIDA ESSEN CARE
GMAN SHEAR ARAP
MOTHERCOURAGE
FEWER ELL DON
ALE ARIA TRENT
DISC ENDEARS
ATLANTABRAVES
OTTOMAN PILL
ADAPT SNOB GOO
PER IDA ASHEN
PRINCEVALIANT
LISA NEVER AERO
EVES TRITE FEET
SENT STATS UNDO
```

18

```
PEPUP SCORE COY
HOUSE MANIA UNA
INFER INTERVIEW
FRICTIONLESS
AMI AHS TITO
RANSOMS ABS NAN
REGLUE GREASERS
OILSPILLS
LUBEJOBS ALTARS
ANE ATA ABYSSES
BILK UNO AVA
SLIPPERYROCK
JOHNRAMBO FRITO
ONO ELMAN FATAL
ESP PLANE SWEDE
```

19

```
SNAP SSTS BARNS
HERE TARO SLOOP
EXCALIBUR AMUSE
STS ELECT ANEW
DEERE HAND
ASKERS BELATED
LEIS AMERICANA
BIN CAMELOT BRR
UNGALLANT SLOT
MEANIES GRUELS
RIPS SCRAM
MOTS CLEAN YDS
ASHES HOLYGRAIL
CLUES ISLE ALLI
HORDE THOR WELD
```

20

```
GRAS AFRO FLOP
RIGA WRAPS RARE
ICEBREAKER ONCE
PEDRO CENT SEAR
ATAT EAST
SLUSHFUND PIANO
HEN SARI CANTOR
ITCH SENTA GAVE
PALEST OONA LEO
STEAK SNOWBALLS
DIAM TEAM
ERIC LULL SURFS
MOTO FREEZESOUT
IDOL AFIRE ELSA
TEND SASE DEER
```

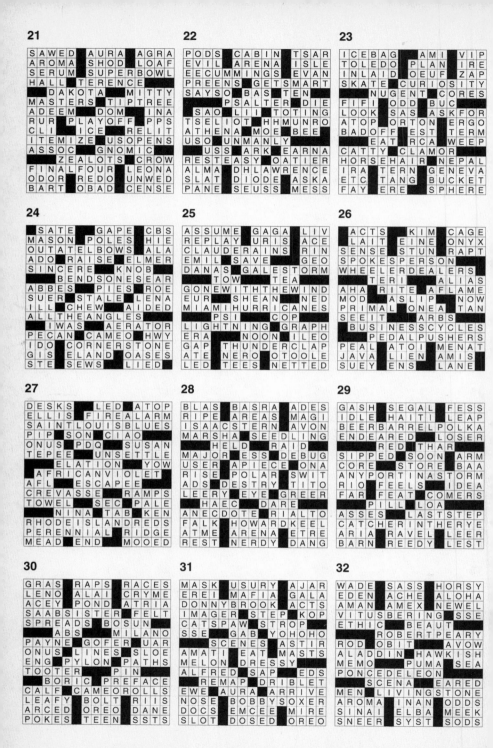

21
```
S A W E D   A U R A   A G R A
A R O M A   S H O D   L O A F
S E R U M   S U P E R B O W L
H A L L   T E R E N C E
    D A K O T A   M I T T Y
M A S T E R S   T I P T R E E
A D E E M   D O M   I N A
R U R   P L A Y O F F   P P S
C L I   I C E   R E L I T
I T E M I Z E   U S O P E N S
A S S O C   G N O M I C
    Z E A L O T S   C R O W
F I N A L F O U R   L E O N A
O D O R   R E D O   U N W E D
B A R T   O B A D   C E N S E
```

22
```
P O D S   C A B I N   T S A R
E V I L   A R E N A   I S L E
E E C U M M I N G S   E V A N
P R E E N S   G E T S M A R T
S A Y S O   B A S   T E N
    P S A L T E R   D I E
S A O   L I I   T O T I N G
T S E L I O T   H H M U N R O
A T H E N A   M O E   B E E
U S O   U N M A N L Y
    U S S   A R K   E A R N A
R E S T E A S Y   O A T I E R
A L M A   D H L A W R E N C E
S L A T   D I O D E   A S K A
P A N E   S E U S S   M E S S
```

23
```
I C E B A G   A M I   V I P
T O L E D O   P L A N   I R E
I N L A I D   O E U F   Z A P
S K A T E   C U R I O S I T Y
    N U G E N T   C O R E S
F I F I   O D D   B U C
L O O K   S A S   A S K F O R
A T O P   O R T O N   E R G O
B A D O F F   E S T   T E R M
    E A T   R C A   W E E P
C A T T Y   C L A M O R
H O R S E H A I R   N E P A L
I R A   T E R N   G E N E V A
E T C   T A N G   B U C K E T
F A Y   E R E   S P H E R E
```

24
```
    S A T E   G A P E   C B S
M A S O N   P O L E S   H I E
O U T A T E L B O W S   A L A
A D O   R A I S E   E L M E R
S I N C E R E   K N O B
    B E N D S O N E S E A R
A B B E S   P I E S   R O E
S U E R   S T A L E   L E N A
I L L   C H E W   A I D E D
A L L T H E A N G L E S
    I W A S   A E R A T O R
P E C A N   C A M E O   H W Y
I D O   C O R N E R S T O N E
G I S   E L A N D   O A S E S
S T E   S E W S   L I E D
```

25
```
A S S U M E   G A G A   L I V
R E P L A Y   U R I S   A C E
C L A U D E R A I N S   R I N
E M I L   S A V E   G E O
D A N A S   G A L E S T O R M
    T O W   T E A
G O N E W I T H T H E W I N D
E U R   S H E A N   N E D
M I A M I H U R R I C A N E S
    P S I   C O P
L I G H T N I N G   G R A P H
E R A   N O O N   I L E O
G A P   T H U N D E R C L A P
A T E   N E R O   O T O O L E
L E D   T E E S   N E T T E D
```

26
```
A C T S   K I M   C A G E
L A I T   E I N E   O N Y X
S E N S E   S T U N   R A P T
S P O K E S P E R S O N
W H E E L E R D E A L E R S
    T E R I   A L I A S
A H A   R I T E   A F L A M E
M O D   A S L I P   N O W
P R I M A L   O N E A   T A N
S E E I T   A R B S
B U S I N E S S C Y C L E S
P E D A L P U S H E R S
P E A L   A T O I   M E N A T
J A V A   L I E N   A M I S
S U E Y   E N S   L A N E
```

27
```
D E S K S   L E D   A T O P
E L L I S   F I R E A L A R M
S A I N T L O U I S B L U E S
P I P   S O N   C I A O
O N U S   P D Q   S U S A N
T E P E E   U N S E T T L E
    E L A T I O N   Y O W
A F R I C A N V I O L E T
A F L   E S C A P E E
C R E V A S S E   R A M P S
T O W E L   S E C   P A L E
    N I N A   T A B   K E N
R H O D E I S L A N D R E D S
P E R E N N I A L   R I D G E
M E A D   E N D   M O O E D
```

28
```
B L A S   B A S R A   A D E S
R I P E   A R E A S   M A G I
I S A A C S T E R N   A V O N
M A R S H A   S E E D L I N G
    H E L D   R A I D
M A J O R   E S S   D E B U G
U S E R   A P I E C E   O N A
R I S E   P O L A R   S W I T
A D S   D E S T R Y   T I T O
L E E R Y   E Y E   G R E E R
    H A E C   D A R E
A N E C D O T E   R I A L T O
F A L K   H O W A R D K E E L
A T M E   A R E N A   E T R E
R E S T   N E R D Y   D A N G
```

29
```
G A S H   S E G A L   F E S S
I D L E   H A I T I   L E A P
B E E R B A R R E L P O L K A
E N D E A R E D   L O S E R
    R E D   T H A R
S I P P E D   S O O N   A R M
C O R E   S T O R E   B A A
A N Y P O R T I N A S T O R M
R I O   F E E L S   I D E A
F A R   F E A T   C O M E R S
    P I L L   L O A
A S S E S   L A S T S T E P
C A T C H E R I N T H E R Y E
A R I A   R A V E L   L E E R
B A R N   R E E D Y   L E S T
```

30
```
G R A S   R A P S   R A C E S
L E N O   A L A I   C R Y M E
A C E Y   P O N D   A T R I A
S A A B S I S T E R   F E L T
S P R E A D S   B O S U N
    A B S   M I L A N O
P A Y N E   G O F E R   U A R
O N U S   L I N E S   S L O E
E N G   P Y L O N   P A T H S
T O O T E R   P I N
    B O R I C   P R E F A C E
C A L F   C A M E O R O L L S
L E A F Y   B O L T   R I I S
A R C E D   O R E O   D A N E
P O K E S   T E E N   S S T S
```

31
```
M A S K   U S U R Y   A J A R
E R E I   M A F I A   G A L A
D O N N Y B R O O K   A C T S
I M A G E R   S T E P   K O P
C A T S P A W   S T R O P
S S E   G A B   Y O H O H O
    S C E N E S   A S T I R
A M A T I   E A T   M A S T S
M E L O N   D R E S S Y
A L F R E D   S A P   E D S
    R E M A P   D R I B L E T
E W E   A U R A   A R R I V E
N O S E   B O B B Y S O X E R
D O C S   E M C E E   M I R E
S L O T   D O S E D   O R E O
```

32
```
W A D E   S A S S   H O R S Y
E D E N   A C H E   A L O H A
A M A N   A M E X   N E W E L
V I T U S B E R I N G   S S E
E T H I C   B E A U T
R O B E R T P E A R Y
R O D   O B I T   A V O W
A L A D D I N   H A W K I S H
M E M O   P U M A   S E A
P O N C E D E L E O N
    S C E N A   E A R E D
M E N   L I V I N G S T O N E
A R O M A   I N A N   O D D S
S I N A I   E L B A   M E E K
S N E E R   S Y S T   S O D S
```

33

```
M O N A . S A R A H . B A W L
O R A L . E R O D E . A S I A
S E V E N D E A D L Y S I N S
T O Y . E G A D . P O I S E S
. . . A G E S . B M W S . . .
P A M P A S . D E A L . B B C
A B O R T . C O A T . P L E A
T H R E E M U S K E T E E R S
T O N S . A R E S . A S S E T
Y R S . K R I S . K N O T T S
. . . F A K E . L I D S . . .
A S S A Y S . V I N E . I Q S
T E N C O M M A N D M E N T S
M E A T . E A S E L . S K I T
E R G S . N E E D Y . T S P S
```

34

```
E S S E S . S E L F . G E M S
L U C R E . I D E O . A L I T
B E R E T . N E A R . M I L A
A T E . T H U N D E R B O L T
. . . W A L E S . M I L T I E
R O B B E R . T H A N E . . .
O P A L . D A R I N G . B O W
O I L E R . V A N . S A R G E
M E L . E J E C T S . D A L E
. . . A V E R T . A M A Z E D
S T A T U E . S W A M I . . .
W A S H E R W O M A N . L S U
A S W E . E R L E . T I N A S
S T A N . R I G A . L O U S E
H E N S . S T A R . E N T E R
```

35

```
. E B R O . A L D A . R E A P
S N E E R . S E A S . A N Y A
I T S Y B I T S Y S P I D E R
D O E S . S I S S I E S . . .
E M T . F A N . G L A N C E .
A B S O R B . T U N E . O A R
. . . T E E D U P . A N K A .
L I T T L E B O Y B L U E . .
. D I N O . P A N E L S . . .
O F F . U M P S . L O O K E R
G E O R G E . T L C . O N O .
. . . A L L E G R O . S O T S
W E E W I L L I E W I N K I E
O V A L . O L G A . L A I R S
W E T S . W A I T . E P E E .
```

36

```
P E L T . . M A I L . S W A T
O N O R . R A N D Y . I A G O
A O N E . A S T E R . S T O P
C L E A R T H E A I R . E G O
H A R D E R . S C O U R . . .
. . . L O A N S . S A N D E R
F I F E . C O A T . M O O L A
A R I . G E R B I L S . G E T
L O R N E . A I D E . A S E A
K N E E L S . N E G E V . . .
. . . B O I L S . I R I D I C
C A R . D O W N T O E A R T H
A L A S . P A E A N . T A M E
R A N T . P L O P S . O M A R
A N D Y . Y E N S . . R A Y E
```

37

```
A N T E . S T O O D . C H A D
C O O T . O R I B I . R I G A
H I G H T A I L I T . I T E M
E R A S U R E S . T A S T E S
. . . N E D . L Y M P H . . .
C A M B E R . B E B E . E D S
A W A R D . C U T A N D R U N
B A K E . S H R U G . R O L E
B R E A K C A M P . P E A C E
Y E T . O O N A . M A D D E R
. . . R E B U T . S A O . . .
S T A R E R . S T I L E T T O
C O C O . G E T A M O V E O N
A R K S . E L A T E . E L S E
B A S E . S I R E D . N E S S
```

38

```
E B B S . B O A R D . D D A Y
R E N E . A L L E Y . E R I E
G E A R . N I E C E . T U R N
F I E L D O F D R E A M S . .
. . . N O S . S C I . . . . .
C A G E R . P E R . U N B A R
O C R . N A I L E D . E R G O
T H E B A D N E W S B E A R S
T E A R . D E N O T E . S E E
A S T O P . D A N . L O S E S
. . . . . W I L . S L R . . .
. . C A S E Y A T T H E B A T
M A G I . R O M E O . I R I S
O P E N . I N A N E . T U N A
B E R G . C E N T S . S T E W
```

39

```
A C H E . . S P A . . C E L T
N O O K . S P E N T . A D A M
N I N E . C R A N E . N A V E
O L E . T H E C A N D Y M A N
. . . Y A H W E H . D U O . .
D A H L I A . . R E F U S A L
A T O M S . S M U R F . U S O
T O N S . D A M N S . A G I N
E N E . W I N E S . B L A D E
R E Y N A R D . . P O O R E R
. . . E R N . P L U S E S . .
S W E E T D R E A M S . U A R
L A R D . L E T U P . O G R E
A K I N . S E A R S . F A I L
M E E T . . F L A . . F R A Y
```

40

```
T W I G . P L E A D . E G G S
O R C A . L E A S E . J I L T
S A K S F I F T H A V E N U E
S P Y . R A T S . D E C A M P
. . . P O N Y . C H E T . . .
A B J E C T . B A E R . J O B
C R E A K . O L G A . G O B I
H I L L S T R E E T B L U E S
E E L S . O B E Y . L A S S O
D R Y . S N I P . L I S T E N
. . . M E E T . B E T S . . .
A G E O L D . M O T H . C H I
M I D D L E O F T H E R O A D
O B I E . A L O H A . D A Z E
S E E M . F E R A L . A X E S
```

41

```
A S U . S P R A T . G W E N
B O N D . E R I C A . R A R E
A U T O G R A P H S . E S T A
S P I L L . T E E S . C H E R
E Y E L I N E R . E P I C . .
. . . A B A . A L L A Y E D .
M S G R . M E N D . U N C L E
O U R . B U S B O Y S . L A B
O R A T E . P A G O . B E N T
. R E V E L R Y . G P O . . .
. . Y A L E . T R A I N E E S
D A B S . A E R O . S I D L E
O B O E . P L A N E A N G L E
L I A R . E L I D E . G A I N
L E T S . R A T O N . R E O .
```

42

```
C A R T . U N P I L E . D D T
O B I E . S E A S O N . R O E
P U L L T H E P L U G . O W L
S T E E R E D . I M P E L . .
. . . C A R . D E N I A L S .
D E C A Y S . D E M E A N . .
A M A S S . L E W I S . C A D
L I L T . R E F E R . A H O Y
E L L . C O V E Y . K R O N E
. . I S O M E R . S O A R E D
. M A T I N E E . T A P . . .
A T A R I . S O L A C E S . .
M I D . C O M E T O A H A L T
A L A . A S T R A L . O S L O
S T Y . L E V E R S . S H A W
```

43

```
C A S H . F A D E . . S M O G
A S H E . A H A I R . C I T E
S H O R T R A N G E . A N T E
T E N D E R . S H A . R I O S
S N E E R . D E T R A C T . .
. . . R I P E . S H E R E E .
L A B S . S A R A . E R A S E
I R A . T I N Y T I M . C P L
F I B E R . S E L L . S K Y S
. T A Y L O R . A L M A . . .
. . B E D E C K S . O V A L S
T A L C . E R A . F R I D A Y
A B U T . L I T T L E N E C K
P E E R . S E I N E . G L E E
E L S A . S E N D . . S A Y S
```

44

```
L O C O . P R A M . J A B E Z
A V O N . T O D O . A S O N E
M E N U . A B E L I N C O L N
R D S . B L E D . A K A . . .
A D E . R Y E . E M P I R E .
S U M A C S . M A Y . E G O .
H E N R Y V I I I . R I S E N
. . . P A P A S M U R F . . .
H E M A N . S M I T H B R O S
U M A . I N K . I S Y O U R .
M A R A C A . S A L . M T S .
. . . N I L . R I T Z . B A T
S A N T A C L A U S . A N A G
A T E A M . K Y R A . I C K Y
G E R R Y . A S E C . T E E M
```

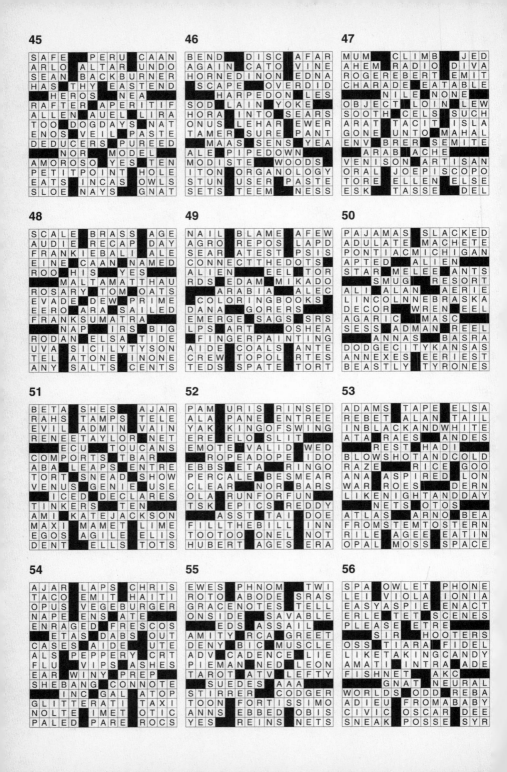

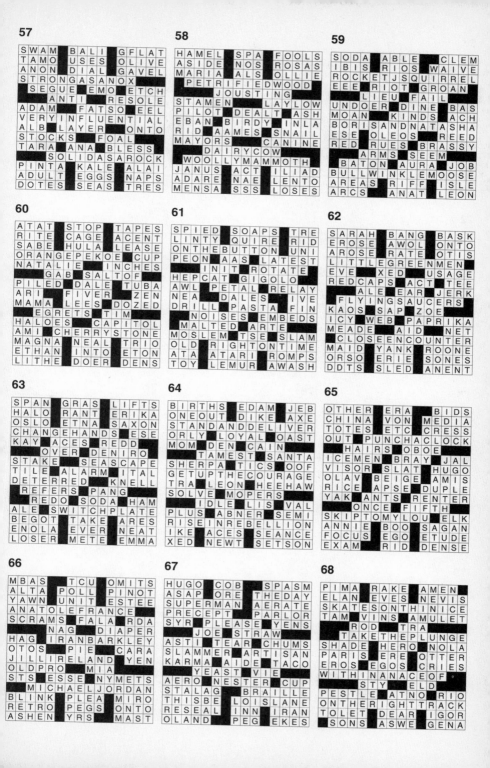

57

```
SWAM BALI  GFLAT
TAMO USES  OLIVE
ANON DIAL  GAVEL
STRONGASANOX
   SEGUE EMO ETCH
     ANTI RESOLE
ADAM  FATSO   EEL
VERYINFLUENTIAL
ALB  LAYER  ONTO
STOCKS  FOAL
TARA  ANA  BLESS
  SOLIDASAROCK
PINTA KALE  ALAI
ADULT EGGS  NAPS
DOTES SEAS  TRES
```

58

```
HAMEL  SPA  FOOLS
ASIDE  NOS  ROSAS
MARIA  ALS  OLLIE
  PETRIFIEDWOOD
     JOUSTING
STAMEN   LAYLOW
PILOT DEALT  ASH
EBAN  BIRDY  INLA
RID  AAMES  SNAIL
MAYORS   CANINE
    DAIRYCOW
WOOLLYMAMMOTH
JANUS  ACT  ILIAD
ADARE  NAE  LENTO
MENSA  SSS  LOSES
```

59

```
SODA  ABLE   CLEM
IBIS  RIOS  WAIVE
ROCKETJSQUIRREL
EEE  RIOT  GROAN
     LIEU  FAIL
UNDOER DINE  BAS
MOAN  KINDS   ACH
BORISANDNATASHA
ESE  OLEOS   REED
RED  RUES  BRASSY
    ARMS  SEEM
BATON  AURA   JOB
BULLWINKLEMOOSE
AREAS RIFF  ISLE
ARCS  ANAT  LEON
```

60

```
ATAT  STOP  TAPES
RITE  CAGE  ACENT
SABE  HULA  LEASE
ORANGEPEKOE  CUP
NATALIE   INCHES
  GAB  SALTOF
PILED DALE  TUBA
ARI  FIVER   ZEN
MAMA  LEES  DOZED
EGRETS   TIM
HALOES  CAPITOL
AMI  CHERRYSTONE
MAGNA NEAL  TRIO
ETHAN INTO  ETON
LITHE DOER  DENS
```

61

```
SPIED  SOAPS  TRE
LINTY  QUIRE  RID
ONTHEBUTTON  UNI
PEON  AAS  LATEST
     INIT  ROTATE
HEPCAT  GIGOLO
AWL  PETAL  RELAY
NEA  DALES   IVE
DRILL PASTA   FIN
  NOISES EMBEDS
MALTED   ARTE
MOSLEM  TSE  SLAM
OLD  RIGHTONTIME
ATA  ATARI  ROMPS
TOY  LEMUR  AWASH
```

62

```
SARAH  BANG   BASK
EROSE  AWOL   ONTO
AROSE  RATE   OTIS
LITTLEGREENMEN
EVE  XED   USAGE
REDCAPS ACT   TEE
   ALE  EAR  JERK
FLYINGSAUCERS
KAOS  SAP   ZOE
ICY  WEB  PAPRIKA
MEADE  AID    NET
CLOSEENCOUNTER
MAID  YANK  ROONE
ORSO  ERIE  SONES
DDTS  SLED  ANENT
```

63

```
SPAN  GRAS  LIFTS
HALO  RANT  ERIKA
OSLO  ETNA  SAXON
CHANGEHANDS  ESE
KAY  ACES   REDD
   OVER  DENIRO
STAKE   SEASCAPE
TILE  ALARM  ITAL
DETERRED   KNELL
REFERS   PANG
REDO  SODA   HAM
ALE  SWITCHPLATE
BEGOT TAKE  ARES
ENOLA EVER  NEAT
LOSER METE  EMMA
```

64

```
BIRTHS  EDAM   JEB
ONEOUT  DIKE   AXE
STANDANDDELIVER
ORLY  LOYAL  OAST
MOM  DEN   CAIN
   TAMEST  SANTA
SHERPA TICS   OOF
GETUPTHECOURAGE
TRA  LEON  HEEHAW
SOLVE   MOPERS
IDLE  LIS   VAL
PLUS  ABNER  SEMI
RISEINREBELLION
IKE  ACES  SEANCE
XED  NEWT  SETSON
```

65

```
OTHER  ERA   BIDS
CHINA  VON  MEDIA
TOTES  ETC  CRESS
OUT  PUNCHACLOCK
   HAIRS  OBOE
ICEMEN  BRAY  JAL
VISOR  SLAT  HUGO
OLAV  BEIGE  AMIS
RICE  APSE  DUPLE
YAK  ANTS  RENTER
   ONCE  FIFTH
SKIPTOMYLOU  ELK
ANNIE  BOO  SAGAN
FOCUS  EGO  ETUDE
EXAM  RID  DENSE
```

66

```
MBAS  TCU   OMITS
ALTA  POLL  PINOT
YAWN  UNIT  ESTEE
ANATOLEFRANCE
SCRAMS FALA   RDA
   NAG  DIAPER
HAG  IRANBARKLEY
OTOS  PIE   CARA
JILLIRELAND  YEN
OLDPRO   MIA
STS  ESSE  NYMETS
  MICHAELJORDAN
BLINK PLEA  MIRO
RETRO PEGS  ONTO
ASHEN YRS   MAST
```

67

```
HUGO  COB   SPASM
ASAP  ORE  THEDAY
SUPERMAN   AERATE
PRECEPT   PARLOR
SYR  PLEASE  YENS
     JOE  STRAW
ASTI  TEAR  CHUMS
SLAMMER   ARTISAN
KARMA  AIDE  TACO
   YEAST   VIE
AERO  NESTER  CUP
STALAG   BRAILLE
THISBE  LOISLANE
RESEAL INN   IRAN
OLAND  PEG   EKES
```

68

```
PIMA  RAKE   AMEN
ELAN  EVES  NEVIS
SKATESONTHINICE
TAM  VINS  AMULET
     ROD   TRA
  TAKETHEPLUNGE
SHADE  HERO  NOLA
PARIS  ERE  OTTER
EROS  EGOS  CRIES
WITHINANACEOF
     STY  ELD
PESTLE  ATNO   RIO
ONTHERIGHTTRACK
TOLET DEAR  IGOR
SONS  ASWE  GENA
```

69

```
■ T I P ■ V E R B ■ R A T E S
L I R E ■ O V A L ■ E R O D E
I D E A ■ L A R A ■ T A T A R
M A S C ■ C H E R R Y B O M B
A L T H E A ■ R E A P ■ ■ ■
■ ■ Y A N K ■ ■ D E G R E E
W O R K R O O M S ■ D R A W N
A L O E ■ S P E E D ■ A C E D
R I S E S ■ S T R I P P E R S
M O A N E D ■ ■ F O R E ■ ■
■ ■ ■ C O T S ■ C O V E R T
A P P L E S A U C E ■ I L I E
B A R E D ■ X M A S ■ N A V E
E L I T E ■ C U R E ■ E T A S
T E X A S ■ O P T S ■ S E L
```

70

```
I Q T E S T ■ H A N D B O O K
S U I T O R ■ A R G U A B L E
H O P A L O N G C A S S I D Y
■ ■ ■ L E T A ■ H I T ■ ■ ■
I F S ■ ■ H U L L O ■ F A D E
B L U R B ■ G A Y ■ E N O S
M O N A R C H Y ■ G A D G E T
■ ■ S K I P T O M Y L O U ■ ■
R A P I E R ■ V A P O R I Z E
A M O S ■ L E N ■ E A S E L
M Y T H ■ D O R I A ■ H E M
■ ■ ■ B O G ■ A S A P ■ ■ ■
J U M P I N J A C K F L A S H
O P E R A H A T ■ E R O D E S
T I R E S O M E ■ R O D E N T
```

71

```
S P A R ■ P A R T ■ S K A T E
L A V E ■ O B O E ■ P I L E S
U S I A ■ L Y N X ■ E C L A T
S H A R P A S A T A C K ■ ■
H A N G A R S ■ ■ N I S S A N
■ ■ U P I ■ S H E A ■ H B O
W I S E A S A N O W L ■ A H S
I D O ■ ■ S E R ■ ■ R O E
S I B ■ F R E E A S A B I R D
P O E ■ R E A R ■ P O O ■ ■
S T R E E T ■ ■ M E N T O R S
■ ■ M A D A S A W E T H E N
S N A C K ■ L O N E ■ L A M A
P U R E E ■ M S G R ■ E R I K
A N T E D ■ S O Y S ■ R A T E
```

72

```
C H I C ■ A D Z E ■ A B B O T
L E N O ■ C O I N ■ N O O N E
I N C L E M E N T ■ T O D A Y
C R O O N E R C R O S B Y ■
H Y M N S ■ ■ A M Y ■ S I P
E V E ■ J U M P Y ■ J U N O
■ ■ U N I F Y ■ ■ T O R T S
F L A S H G O R D O N S F O E
L E V E L ■ ■ N O R T H ■ ■
A V E R ■ I S A A C ■ G A B
K I M ■ A S P ■ M A U V E
■ A U T H O R L A R D N E R
H A R P O ■ N E O N T E T R A
A X I O M ■ G A W K ■ P E S T
M E A N S ■ E L S A ■ T R E E
```

73

```
N O T E ■ P A S S E ■ S W A M
A M I N ■ O R C A S ■ P E S O
P I L L O W T A L K ■ O T T O
A T T I R E ■ N A I R O B I
■ ■ V A L E T ■ M I L L ■ ■
S H E L L S ■ B O N S A I S
A T O N ■ S T R E S S ■ N R A
B E T S Y ■ E A R ■ O N K E Y
I N S ■ I D R E A M ■ E E N S
T O P P E R S ■ T O D A T E
■ ■ R O L E ■ T E N O R ■ ■
W I N D S O R ■ S O N A T A
T O N I ■ S H E E T M E T A L
U R G E ■ E T A G E ■ S A L T
B E S S ■ R O T O R ■ S T L O
```

74

```
B A C H ■ S P O T ■ ■ E N O S
A C R E ■ T I B I A ■ L A P P
T H E M O R N I N G A F T E R
H E W ■ D I K E ■ I D I O C Y
■ ■ ■ B E V Y ■ S T A N ■
R E B A T E ■ B E A M ■ S S T
O P A R T ■ B E A T ■ I N T O
D O G D A Y A F T E R N O O N
I C E S ■ A S I S ■ E L O P E
N H L ■ B R I T ■ A V A T A R
■ M A D E ■ S L A W ■ ■ ■
S H E I L A ■ A H E M ■ V I I
M I D N I G H T E X P R E S S
U R I S ■ E A R L E ■ O R A L
G E E K ■ M A L I ■ T Y K E
```

75

```
A V A ■ ■ M A T E S ■ P H I L
L I M P ■ O R A L S ■ R A R E
A T O R ■ D E B I T H O M A S
M A N O R I A L ■ ■ O N S E T
P E G G Y F L E M I N G ■ ■
■ ■ R E Y ■ ■ A R I ■ L O A
O G R E ■ ■ D A M N D E S T
K R I S T I Y A M A G U C H I
L E T S I N O N ■ ■ C H A T
A W E ■ R I D ■ S E T ■ ■
■ ■ K A T A R I N A W I T T
A L O O N ■ A C E T O N E S
S O N J A H E N I E ■ R O N A
T A T A ■ A N G E R ■ K N A R
A M O K ■ L E E R S ■ E M S
```

76

```
A J A R ■ S C A M ■ P L I E S
R O S E ■ T R E E ■ R I F L E
I T S S O E A S Y ■ O L I V E
■ ■ ■ I M S O E X C I T E D
L A M A S ■ S P R E E ■ S S S
A T O N E S ■ D E L ■ ■
B E S S ■ O K R A ■ D A M S
S H E S S O U N U S U A L
T E L L ■ S N A P ■ D U O S
■ ■ M A Y ■ ■ S L E D G E
A K C ■ V E N O M ■ I R E S T
Y O U R E S O V A I N ■ ■
E A T E R ■ H E S S O F I N E
A L I N E ■ O T O E ■ A V I S
R A T E D ■ W A N E ■ T E X T
```

77

```
E R I N ■ A T E S T ■ A J A R
G O R E ■ W A S T E ■ T A B U
G U M W R A P P E R ■ O W E S
S E A T E R ■ ■ T R E M B L E
■ ■ O P E R A ■ E M I R ■
B A R N S ■ O D E ■ O C E A N
E L I S ■ G I M L E T ■ A G O
L I V ■ F O L I A T E ■ K I D
L E E ■ I B E R I A ■ P E L E
E N R O L ■ D A N ■ P A R E S
■ M U T E ■ L E G I T ■ ■
S M O T H E R ■ ■ A T T I C S
P O U R ■ L I P S T H E C U P
E T T U ■ E L I T E ■ R E B A
C O H N ■ D E G A S ■ S R A S
```

78

```
W A L D O ■ P A L M ■ C A S K
O R I O N ■ A L O E ■ A N T E
R U M P E L S T I L T S K I N
K N E E ■ E T O N ■ H E A R T
■ ■ S L A Y ■ C L A Y ■ ■
P Y T H O N ■ B L O W ■ P A M
A A H E D ■ F O O L ■ S A N E
T H R E E L I T T L E P I G S
C O O T ■ A R C H ■ T I N E S
H O W ■ J O S H ■ B A K E R Y
■ ■ H O S T ■ P O L E ■ ■
C L A U S ■ L I A R ■ H E N S
H A N S E L A N D G R E T E L
O I N K ■ O D O R ■ M E T O O
P R E Y ■ T Y N E ■ S L U N G
```

79

```
T O M ■ ■ S T A L L ■ M A P S
A N A T ■ W Y L I E ■ A L T O
M A G I ■ A R E N A ■ C L O Y
R E M O T E C O N T R O L ■
N O N E W S ■ ■ S H O V E L
E L T O N ■ P G A ■ E N E M Y
O L A F ■ C H A L E T ■ R Y E
■ ■ F A R O U T M A N ■ ■
A B E ■ B I N G E S ■ O T T O
H O M E R ■ E E R ■ S M I R K
A N I M A L ■ ■ S P I N E S
■ F R O M A D I S T A N C E
F I A T ■ N O L T E ■ E A T S
A R T E ■ E V I A N ■ E N O L
N E E D ■ S E E N O ■ S P Y
```

80

```
R O B E R T ■ P O L O ■ S K Y
O N E T O O ■ L I O N ■ H I E
M A R C U S W E L B Y ■ O N S
P I E ■ E S A U ■ X E R ■
S R T A ■ P Y R E S ■ S T I R
■ ■ L E O N A R D M C C O Y
E L A T E ■ A S A R U L E
B R A T S ■ ■ N O T E S
A I R H E A D ■ A V O W S
J A M E S K I L D A R E ■
A L A R ■ A S I A N ■ D E N S
■ R E O ■ A S O F ■ L O A
J F K ■ J O H N H W A T S O N
A L E ■ O D E A ■ E R R A N D
B U D ■ S E W S ■ N O I S E S
```

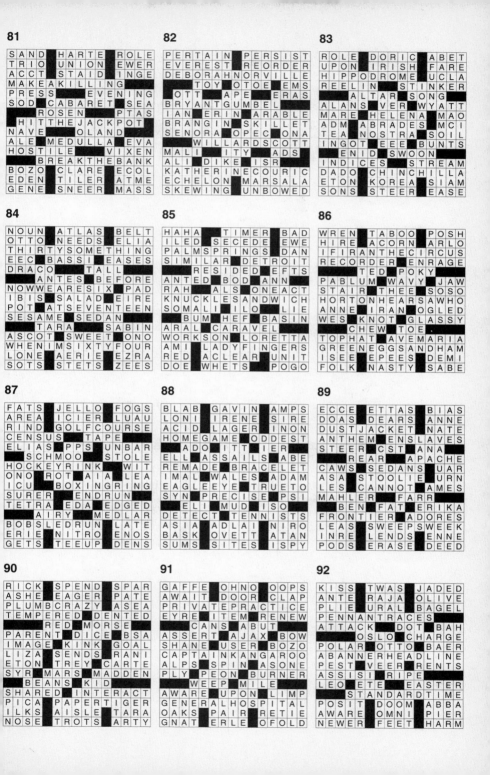

81

SAND · HARTE · ROLE
TRIO · UNION · EWER
ACCT · STAID · INGE
MAKEAKILLING
PRESS · EVENING
SOD · CABARET · SEA
ROSEN · PTAS
HITTHEJACKPOT
NAVE · OLAND
ALE · MEDULLA · EVA
HOSTILE · VIXEN
BREAKTHEBANK
BOZO · CLARE · ECOL
EDEN · TILER · ATME
GENE · SNEER · MASS

82

PERTAIN · PERSIST
EVEREST · REORDER
DEBORAHNORVILLE
TOY · OTOE · EMS
OTT · APE · ERAS
BRYANTGUMBEL
IAN · ERIN · ARABLE
BRANGIN · SKILLET
SENORA · OPEC · ONA
WILLARDSCOTT
MALI · ITY · ADS
ALI · DIKE · ISR
KATHERINECOURIC
ECHELON · MARSALA
SKEWING · UNBOWED

83

ROLE · DORIC · ABET
UPON · IRISH · FARE
HIPPODROME · UCLA
REELIN · STINKER
ALTAR · SONG
ALANS · VER · WYATT
MARE · HELENA · MAO
ADM · ABRADES · MCI
TEA · NOSTRA · SOIL
INGOT · EEE · BUNTS
ENID · SWOON
INDICES · STREAM
DADO · CHINCHILLA
ETON · KOREA · SIAM
SONS · STEER · EASE

84

NOUN · ATLAS · BELT
OTTO · NEEDS · ELIA
THIRTYSOMETHING
EEC · BASSI · EASES
DRACO · TALL
ANTES · BEFORE
NOWWEARESIX · PAD
IBIS · SALAD · EIRE
POT · ATSEVENTEEN
SESAME · SEDAN
TARA · SABIN
ASCOT · SWEET · ONO
WHENIMSIXTYFOUR
LONE · AERIE · EZRA
SOTS · STETS · ZEES

85

HAHA · TIMER · BAD
ILED · SECEDE · EWE
PALMSPRINGS · DAN
SIMILAR · DETROIT
RESIDED · EFTS
ANTED · BOD · ANN
RAH · ALS · ONEACT
KNUCKLESANDWICH
SOMALI · ILO · LIE
BUM · HEF · BASIN
ARAL · CARAVEL
WORKSON · LORETTA
AMI · LADYFINGERS
RED · ACLEAR · UNIT
DOE · WHETS · POGO

86

WREN · TABOO · POSH
HIRE · ACORN · ARLO
IFIRANTHECIRCUS
RECORDER · ENRAGE
TED · POKY
PABLUM · WAVY · JAW
STAIR · THEE · SOSO
HORTONHEARSAWHO
ANNE · IRAN · OGLED
WES · KNOT · GLASSY
CHEW · TOE
TOPHAT · AVEMARIA
GREENEGGSANDHAM
ISEE · EPEES · DEMI
FOLK · NASTY · SABE

87

FATS · JELLO · FOGS
AREA · ICIER · LUAU
RIND · GOLFCOURSE
CENSUS · TAPE
ELIAS · PPS · UNBAR
SCHMOO · STOLE
HOCKEYRINK · WIT
ONO · ROT · AIA · LEA
ICU · BOXINGRING
SURER · ENDRUN
TETRA · EDA · EDGED
AIRY · MEDLAR
BOBSLEDRUN · LATE
ERIE · NITRO · ENOS
GETS · TEEUP · DENS

88

BLAB · GAVIN · AMPS
LONI · IRENE · SIRE
ACID · LAGER · INON
HOMEGAME · ODDEST
ADO · ITT · IER
ELL · ASSAILS · ABE
REMADE · BRACELET
IMAL · WALES · ADAM
EAGLEEYE · TRUETO
SYN · PRECISE · PSI
ELI · MUD · ISO
DETECT · TENNISTS
ASIA · ADLAI · NIRO
BASK · OVETT · ATAN
SUMS · SITES · ISPY

89

ECCE · ETTAS · BIAS
DOAS · DEARS · ANNE
DUSTJACKET · NATE
ANTHEM · ENSLAVES
STEER · CST · ANA
REAR · APACHE
CAWS · SEDANS · UAR
ASA · STOOLIE · URN
LES · CANNOT · AMES
MAHLER · FARR
BEN · FAT · ERIKA
FRONTIER · ADORES
LEAS · SWEEPSWEEK
INRE · LENDS · ENNE
PODS · ERASE · DEED

90

RICK · SPEND · SPAR
ASHE · EAGER · PATE
PLUMBCRAZY · ASEA
TEMPERED · DENTED
RED · MORSE
PARENT · DICE · BSA
IMAGE · KINK · GOAL
LIZA · SENDS · RANI
ETON · TREY · CARTE
SYR · MARS · MADDEN
BEANS · KID
SHARED · INTERACT
PICA · PAPERTIGER
ILKS · AISLE · TARA
NOSE · TROTS · ARTY

91

GAFFE · OHNO · OOPS
AWAIT · DOOR · CLAP
PRIVATEPRACTICE
EYRE · ITEM · RENEW
CANS · ABUT
ASSERT · AJAX · BOW
SHANE · USER · BOZO
CAPTAINKANGAROO
ALPS · SPIN · ASONE
PLY · PEON · BURNER
WEEP · MILE
AWARE · UPON · LIMP
GENERALHOSPITAL
OAKS · PAIR · RETIE
GNAT · ERLE · OFOLD

92

KISS · TWAS · JADED
ANTE · RAJA · OLIVE
PLIE · URAL · BAGEL
PENNANTRACES
ATTACK · DOT · BAH
OSLO · CHARGE
POLAR · OTTO · BAER
ABANNERHEADLINE
PEST · VEER · RENTS
ASSISI · RIPE
LEO · ETE · EASTER
STANDARDTIME
POSIT · DOOM · ABBA
AWARE · OMNI · PIER
NEWER · FEET · HARM

93

```
S H E S   S W A I N   C A K E
E A V E   H O R N E   A N N A
T H E L I O N I N W I N T E R
H A L F N O T E   L O O S E N
      T I S   T Y N E
M A T R O N   M O W S   C B S
O R B I T   P I K E   S A L K
C R O C O D I L E D U N D E E
H O N K   I C O N   N U R S E
A W E   T S K S   A T B E S T
      P O K Y   E R R
S C R I B E   I N C U B A T E
P L A N E T O F T H E A P E S
R E N T   T O W E L   L I R A
Y O K O   E M E R Y   M E N U
```

94

```
T I L D E   P O O R   S R A
O C E A N   U P T O   S T E P
T O N Y C U R T I S   H A V E
S N O C O N E   S T E R N E R
      A R I E S   E V I L L Y
T U R R E T   E U R E K A
K N E E   E V E R   R E U P S
O D D   E S O   G I S   R A H
S O B E R   W R E N   A E R O
  U N R E S T   V A L L E E
P A T T O N   E M I R S
A T T I R E S   A V I A N C A
C R O C   R I N G O S T A R R
T I N E   G L E N   T I B E T
S A S   Y O G A   O A S E S
```

95

```
E R A   J A V A   Y A W N E D
L O M   U R I S   A D R I A N
I C E S T A T I O N Z E B R A
J O C A S T A   U K E S
A C H Y   M I S E   T A C T
H O E   T W I S T E R   C O O
      G R A N T   I N L A W
W A T E R C H E S T N U T
W A G O N   M A I Z E
    L O I S   W I N E R E D
E V E   D E B U S S Y   T W O
B E E P   V E S T   W H E N
S T E A M L O C O M O T I V E
P A S C A L   H O O T   V I C
A R T E R Y   E D N A   E L K
```

96

```
R I D E   G A S P   C O M A
A N O N   T A B O O   O V E R
C A N D L E P I N S   N A N A
E N A M O R   E A T   C L U B
R E S O U N D   R A T E
      S T A R S   G A R A G E
H A R T   L A N T E R N J A W
U S A   W A Y   A L E
L A M P O O N I N G   P R E S
A P P E A R   L A R G E
    D R A G   N E A T A S A
M R E D   C R O   E V A D E S
C O L L   L I G H T E R M E N
A B L E   E L L I S   D I M E
N E E R   S L E D   S T E R
```

97

```
B O R G   M A I M   B I T S
A S I A   B E L L A   O N I T
I S N T   O N A I R   B A R A
R I G H T A S R A I N   B E N
D E S E R T   M C N A I R
    R U M P   E B B E T S
E G G S   A R E A   O N E A L
G E E   S N O W J O B   Z O O
A N T A L   W E A N   P E S T
D E W I E R   R E D O
I M P O S E   E D U C E S
P U N   T A K E B Y S T O R M
A L D A   S I R E E   E R N E
I N O N   T R I E D   R O I L
R A F T   S T E P   S T E T
```

98

```
A S S E S   M A R S   L E T T
T H E M E   A L E C   O L I O
E A T E N   R I T A   G L E N
S P I N D O C T O R   R A R E
T E N D E R   R E N O
      R E A C T   E L A T E
O R B S   G I L   P O L L E N
R E A P   O M E G A   E G A D
E N J O I N   A A R   R A M S
S T A I R   A N T I S
    L E A D   S P R I N T
L E S S   W A R D H E E L E R
A L U M   A G E E   A B O V E
M A M A   S I D E   R U N E S
A N O N   H O O D   S T A R S
```

99

```
T O S C A   H E R O D   S A O
A B H O R   A L I V E   I T S
L O O N E Y T U N E S   L E A
L E O N   E E L   R E F L A G
      O M A R   C A R R Y M E
F A C T O R   R A G T O P
I N R E D   G E N E S   U F O
E T A S   A L O E S   S T E P
F E Z   C R E W S   U T T E R
  Y E O M A N   G R A Y L Y
S A H A R A N   R A I N
A M O U N T   O A R   D A T A
D A R   F U N N Y P A P E R S
A S S   E R A T O   M A R I A
T S E   D E M O N   S T O M P
```

100

```
C H U G   A S M A D   C A S A
R O S Y   R U E D E   A U N T
A H E M   A P T E R   T R I O
B O R N F R E E   E R S A T Z
      A L A R   S L O P
R A I S E T H E T I T A N I C
E M O T E   E X E C   W A S H
N A W   E R U P T   M A I
E T A S   T O R S   G L E A N
S I N K T H E B I S M A R C K
      E W E S   S P A N
P A R L O R   S T A N D P A T
E X I T   E A T E R   S U L U
A L T O   A V E R S   A M E S
L E A N   L A P S E   T A C K
```